Curt Cloninger

One
Per Year

Curt Cloninger
One Per Year

Publisher: LINK Editions, Brescia 2014
www.linkartcenter.eu

Printed and distributed by: Lulu.com
www.lulu.com

ISBN 978-1-291-92372-8

Curt Cloninger is an artist, writer, and currently an Assistant Professor of New Media at the University of North Carolina Asheville (US). His art undermines language as a system of meaning in order to reveal it as an embodied force in the world. His art work has been featured in the *New York Times* and at festivals and galleries worldwide. Exhibition venues include Centre Georges Pompidou (Paris), Granoff Center for The Creative Arts (Brown University), Black Mountain College Museum + Arts Center, and the internet.

Cloninger has written on a wide range of topics, including new media and internet art, installation and performance art, experimental graphic design, popular music, network culture, and continental philosophy. This is his eighth book. He maintains **http://lab404.com**, **http://playdamage.org**, and **http://deepyoung.org** in hopes of facilitating a more lively remote dialogue with the Sundry Contagions of Wonder.

*To my departmental colleagues: Lei Han,
Lorraine Walsh, Susan Reiser, Christopher
Oakley, Peter Kusek, and Tina McCants.
I have enjoyed working with y'all.*

*Thanks to all the original editors,
commissioners, and publishers of these texts:
Nick Briz, Barry Jones, Josephine Berry Slater,
Agam Andreas, Evan Meaney, Rosa Menkman,
William Robertson, Jon Satrom, Jessica
Westbrook, Juan Martin Prada, Iain Kerr, Kevin
Kelly, Jason Killingsworth, Paul St George,
Kevin McGarry, Patrick Lichty, Christiane Paul,
Kris Krug, and Jeffrey Zeldman. And thanks to
the (meta-)editor of this book
Domenico Quaranta.*

_ CURT CLONINGER

Contents

Introduction

This book is based on a web page I maintain called "one per year" <http://lab404.com/oneperyear.html>. The web page includes links to one of my essays per year and one of my art projects per year since 2000. This book contains the essays less the art projects. There are lots more essays and lots more art projects, but the point of "one per year" is to take a representative chronological sample in order to foreground the evolution of my thinking (and my art practice). Since I am thinking about media that is itself evolving, these essays are also a way to track the evolution of the media itself.

I first got online around 1995 from Fairhope, Alabama, US. I initially got on so that I could correspond with the woman who would become my wife. She was going to school six hours away in Gainesville, Georgia, I was poor, and phone calls were too expensive. So we used telnet to type back and forth in realtime. Then for fun, as long as I was online, I started breaking into other people's computer systems via telnet, because it was intellectually challenging. Then I started web designing, because it was almost as intellectually challenging and a lot less illegal. Then I started making internet art (and then new media art, and then just art). Then I started reading continental philosophy. And now I am ruined.

_ Curt Cloninger
May 2014

2014

Sabotage!
Glitch Politix
Man[ual/ifesto]
(With Nick Briz)

Nick Briz and Curt Cloninger talk about Sabotage in Chicago

1

Computers don't make mistakes, people do. If all variables remain the same, given the same input, a computer will always render the same output; however, often times a programmer slips, she forgets to close a loop and/or accidentally leaves a memory leak. Other times a user opens a file in a way they may not have intended and/or he might pull his USB stick before files have finished transferring. These slips result in entirely predictable, yet unexpected output. We tend to place the onus on the computer and call this moment a glitch.

2

Maybe it helps to think of a glitch as an interruption in a system. More pragmatically useful for our purposes is how specifically the contours of the system are revealed upon its interruption. There are a thousand different ways to fail, and each new way enacts a unique (uniquely exploitable) contour of the system's behavior. Heidegger's broken hammer [1] causes us to stop and examine the entire world (all our other cobbler tools, our cobbler bench, shoes, our workshop, the hillside, cow hides, rain, awls, sledgehammers, nintendo entertainment systems), a world we had been using implicitly, a world with which we were entangled unawares. But so what? Stop looking at the broken hammer and break some more hammers. A thousand broken hammers.

3

Maybe it is helpful to think of politics as shared matters of human concern that congregate around things in the world. Things in the world are connected to other things in the world. Indeed, things connected to other things are what make the world. No things, no world. Maybe it is helpful to own this understanding of politics, things, and the world without having to constantly refer back to Latour and Heidegger.

4

A glitch reveals itself as political when it reminds us that technologies are not neutral tools, but rather are symptoms of our worldview and cultural norms: when encryption breaks, leaking user credentials – how have we come to view privacy when Facebook fields feedback into themselves – how have we come to view identity when emails garble and voice/video over IP slip/drop – how have we come to view relationships.

5

"The very conditions that make the State or World war machine possible, in other words constant capital (resources and equipment) and human variable capital, continually recreate unexpected possibilities for counterattack, unforeseen initiatives, determining revolutionary, popular, minority, mutant machines." [2] Indeed, there is no need to fear or hope. There is not even a need to look for new weapons. We just need to tweak the weapons we already have.

6

If politics are simply shared matters of human concern that congregate around things in the world (and they are), then the glitch event, as a thing in the world, is always already inherently political. But then so is toothpaste (and it is).

7

A glitch is [more] political when it's intended to be.

8

We need not create glitches in sterile glitch laboratories and em-
bed them into currently existent world systems. That is muddlehea-
ded modernist thinking. The glitch naturally arises from within our
currently existent, already entangled systems. These systems have
their own technologies, but they also have their own politics, laws,
economics, histories, memories, and possible futures. The anecdotal
wooden shoes were already there on the workers in the factory. They
didn't have to smuggle in their weapons. There is no need for artificially "embedding" saboteurs. We saboteurs are already embedded.

9

"There is a noble tradition throughout architectural history of signature buildings leaking, cracking, or otherwise failing to live up
to the basic necessities of good engineering. Apparently the Stata
Center was suffering from the same fate, for the building began to
fail in various ways, so much so that the university sued Gehry in
2007 for alleged design and construction shortcomings. The irony
is clear: Gehry has built his reputation on a very specific form of
aestheticize breakage, yet here he is blamed for his buildings breaking." [3]

10

There is a difference [in effect] between something that looks
like it's breaking and something which is "honestly" breaking. "Ho-

nest informatic failures – failures of function – if they are pleasu-
rable or 'artistic' in any way, are typically recast under a purely aesthetic aegis. Hence there exist a number of artists creating beauty
via the corruption of function." [4]

11

A glitch is less effective when it's expected.

12

The machine can't recognize a glitch. Only humans recognize a
glitch as a glitch. Because the machine has no cause/effect expec-
tations. It simply does what it does. A glitch is experienced when
a human mis-expects one thing and winds up with something else.
Without hope, anticipation, and expectation, without a sense of
rightness and the way things are supposed to be, there is no glitch.
There are merely events in the world. When humans filter out the
glitch as so much noise interfering with their status quo signal, when
humans refuse to engage with and be thrilled and terrified by the
nuances of the glitch event, they are making a [con/pre]servative
political decision.

13

"The political glitch implies and implicates human bodies.
The last mile of all media is analog – sound waves, light waves,
smell waves, touch waves, the waves of empathetic mirror neu-

rons, the haptic waves of bodies in space. We don't taste in binary. The political glitch travels from silicon machine (still physical hardware) to human wetware, glitching as it goes. Like Tony Conrad's flicker films – the projector doesn't have an epileptic seizure. The glitch happens when the media runs (last mile) on human bodies."

14

The glitch becomes personally political at that very moment when the human experiencing the glitch feels herself implicit in the entangled systems that give rise to the glitch. This is the moment of personal onus, of personal implication, of personal responsibility. Beyond the initial "a-ha" revelatory moment of uncanny tripped-out-ness, and on toward the subsequent "oh shit" moment of personal implication.

15

A glitch is as political as a car door catching a finger; a glitch becomes political when it catches your finger.

16

The path between "a-ha" and "oh shit" can be almost intsantaneous, because the machine accelerates lived time/space affects. The digital visual glitch can have a jarring effect that overcomes our initial "trained" resistances to slower analog affects. Unlike the numbing/narcotic effect of the filmic jump-cut, this glitch jar can affectively slap us into feeling a part of.

17

let's make a distinction between the glitch(y) as in aesthetic [datamosh(y), noise(y), pixel(y), artifact(y)] and the glitch as in the "a-ha" and "oh shit" [break, crack, interruption, slip]. Two different sets of qualities which at times are shared by the same occurrence and at times not.

18

The other day I was skyping with someone... I started losing interest and then the video glitched; I immediately screen captured it... but then, I always do.

19

OR... the path between "a-ha" and "oh shit" can be much more gradual and corrosive. Hours-long, multi-person, multi-location, networked video chat sessions can contain recurring lags, irruptions, interruptions, drop-outs, and feedbacks – until we gradually feel the distances and failures of the time/space network in our bodies, in our language.

20

All glitch art achieves an initial "a-ha" epiphanic moment (by definition, otherwise it would not be "read" by humans as "glitch"). The initial "a-ha" is a given. The implicit "oh shit" takes some doing on the part of the artist. The goal of the "political" glitch artist is to stage/wire/infuse/pre-load her glitch event so that it purposefully unfolds from "a-ha" to "oh shit." The "political" glitch artist is (eventually) dis-satisfied with the production of trippy looking shit. The "political" glitch artist (eventually) seeks to glitch out shit in ways that lead to an implicit awareness of our human/system entanglements, and an implicit onus on the part of the "viewer" to move those entanglements higher up and further in. Political glitch art means to endow its "viewer" with a feeling of her own agency and the heaviness/obligation that accompanies it.

21

If a file corrupts on a server and no one is around to say "oh shit," it does not make a glitch.

22

The "political" glitch artist is lazy like a fox. Code once, run everywhere, always already. She seeks out tipping points, state change thresholds, fulcrums of agency – locations within systems where the least little tweak irrupts in an exponential modulation. She's constantly folding, recursively escalating. Lather, rinse, repeat.

23

That sweet spot of agency, that fulcrum of most-bang-for-the-buck, often lies in the file's source code. Change a file's header and leave the rest of its descriptive information intact. You get a duck that runs like a car. No need to add wheels, just inform the duck it's a car. It's going to crash in a million different ways. Let me count the ways.

24

"Political" glitch art doesn't always "look" glitchy. It isn't always digital. Sometimes you can't even "see" it. You may only hear it or touch it; you'll always at least feel it. Political glitch art is simply a catch and release program for a thousand ghosts in a thousand machines. It foregrounds the funk that was already there, and foregrounds the fact that you were already there too, knee deep in funk.

25

Political glitch art doesn't always involve the machine. Yes, sometimes things start off non-computery and then get massaged via computery processes; and sometimes things start off computery and then get massaged via non-computery processes. Lather, rinse, repeat. But really, there's not a discrete, computery world that exists outside of a discrete, non-computery world. We live in a word, and sometimes that world gets computery. Glitches live and play in the world – alongside computers, bodies, rocks, aunts, sentences, hammers, ideas, and manifestos.

26

Political glitch art must always involve the machine; it is etymo-
logically and culturally a technical occurrence in a biological world.
It is no more the corrupted file than it is the device interpreting the
file than it is the person who is interpreting the device's interpretation of the file. It exists between these things. Glitches didn't exist
before machines and they will cease to exist when the distinction
between people and machines collapses. A glitch is of the times, and
can only be political in the moment.

27

The political glitch refuses to function as a mere signifier, a mere
symbol, a mere glyph of visual language. Maybe it is all those things
also. Who knows? Who cares? It is indifferent to its own semiotic
status. It aims to affectively jar bodies. "No page in history, baby;
that I don't need / I just wanna make some eardrums bleed." [5]

28

There are all sorts of significant differences between glitch sabotage and situationist detournement. Glitch sabotage and situationist
detournement are pretty much the same thing. There are all sorts of
significant differences between glitch sabotage and computer viruses. Glitch sabotage and computer viruses are pretty much the same
thing.

29

A glitch ceases to be political when it becomes a [mere] image.

30

Glitch sabotage occurs when a glitch is sent out into the network in a way that purposefully resists recapture, recontextualization, and normalization. Like a virus, it glitches-up all it contacts, not necessarily technically, but always human-cognitively.

31

How might glitch artists purposefully load/lade their glitches and release them back upstream into and beyond the entangled systems that initially birthed them? What short-circuited explosions might be triggered? What system modulations might such chain-reactions engender?

32

How might glitches be intentionally rigged to {buffer} overflow their containing systems? Within (and without) the machine?

33

The most efficacious glitch art begins to eat away its own frames. Like Glitchr's art on Facebook and Google – his glitched text over-runs the neat div[ision]s and borders of the corporate web. Derrida's parergon gets a second coat of sulfuric acid. Like William Pope L.'s "Black Factory" – a mobile performance unit that takes "black" objects and physically converts them into other objects. The Black Factory is a machine that modulates the "aura" of discrete/singular objects. As an object-modulating machine, it resists being easily transformed into an object (via art-historical canonization or institutional archiving). The Black Factory effectively throws a boot into any institutional machine that wishes to transform it into an object. In the archiving process, said institutional machine is immediately revealed for what it is (A Memory Factory? A Culture Factory? A sterilization factory?). The Black Factory intentionally self-sabotages its own eventual/inevitable recontextualization as an archived art object.

34

Political glitch art passes through the systems of the world, and in so passing, it exposes, resists, problematizes, confounds, and ultimately transforms the way in which the systems of the world function.

35

There is no pure, clear, clean, natural, normal, transcendental "signal" to be dialed-in. There never has been.

36

"The attempt to regulate and filter out irruptive 'noise' and return to the ideal of a pure signal is the same metaphysical/Platonic attempt to downplay the immanent and maintain (the myth of) the pure transcendent. Subverting... this dichotomous, binary metaphysical system is a radical (root level) 'political' act... [Political] glitch art is not merely 'symbolic' of a politics of noise tolerance... [It] doesn't merely 'symbolize' a political stance; it actively practices one."

37

"Presentation... is presented in its very inadequation, adequate to its inadequation. The inadequation of presentation is presented." [6] Visual political glitch art takes "symbolic," mimetic, figurative visuals and places them under performative erasure. The visual glitch image is the trace which remains, flickering in limbo between figuration and abstraction. The visual glitch (often) makes present the process of digital re-presentation, while still leaving a remnant of the "source" image visible. The glitch image is a fecund remainder rather than an impotent/naught remainder, a remainder that makes visible the violence inherent in the system. (Come and see the violence inherent in the system.)

38

plz gltch this.man[ual/ifesto]

///

This man[ual/ifesto] originally appeared in the catalog for "Tactical Glitches" (SUDLAB Contemporary Art, Naples, Italy), January 2014. Also available online at <www.tacticalgl.it/ches/txt/sabotage.html>

[1] [Editor's note] The "broken hammer" is an example introduced by Martin Heidegger to explain the concept of "presence at hand". Cf. *Wikipedia*, <http://en.wikipedia.org/wiki/Heideggerian_terminology>: "Presence-at-hand is not the way things in the world are usually encountered, and it is only revealed as a deficient or secondary mode, e.g., when a hammer breaks it loses its usefulness and appears as merely there, present-at-hand. When a thing is revealed as present-at-hand, it stands apart from any useful set of equipment but soon loses this mode of being present-at-hand and becomes something, for example, that which must be repaired or replaced."
[2] Gilles Deleuze, Félix Guattari, *A Thousand Plateaus*, Continuum Books / University of Minnesota, 2004 (1987). Trans. Brian Massumi, p. 465.
[3] Alexander R. Galloway, *The Interface Effect*, Polity Press, Malden (MA) 2012, pp. 94 - 95.
[4] Ibid., p. 96.
[5] From the song "Heavy Duty", by Spinal Tap (*Back From The Dead*, 2009).
[6] Jacques Derrida, *The Truth in Painting*, trans. Geoff Bennington and Ian McLeod (Chicago and London: University of Chicago Press, 1987), pp. 131 - 132.

2013
On Lying

Famous lying art vs. unfamous true non-art: Harry Shunk, *Man In Space! The Painter of Space Throws Himself into the Void!*, 1960. Published in *Dimanche, Newspaper for a Single Day*, November 27, 1960

A while back I wrote a book on how to be creative. It was bound to fail because creativity doesn't really break down into easy modernist steps like a recipe you can follow. Indeed, something like "individual human creativity" arguably doesn't even really exist. It's just an idea humans invented at a particular time in history to make them feel good about being humans at that particular time in history. Even so, great artistic chefs do use recipes, and failure sometimes leads to fruitful art, so it wasn't such a bad idea to write a book like that after all. The book was like a way for me to exhaust all the "best practice" advice on how to be creative, compile it in a single text, get it out of my system, and then whatever was left after that might actually have something to do with creativity.

So I researched all sorts of methods for being creative, and distilled them into a long list. Here are a bunch of those methods:

repeat, combine, add, transfer, empathize, animate, superimpose, change scale, fragment, isolate, distort, disguise, contradict, parody, analogize, hybridize, metamorphose, substitute, simplify, adapt, modify, rearrange, reverse, symbolize, mythologize, fantasize.

Finally, my favorite method is "prevaricate," which simply means "lie." I love the prevaricate method and find it woefully underused by artists (although politicians use it all the time). I'm not sure why artists' don't lie more in their work. If you make art involving networks, then the medium more or less forces your work to lie, whether you want it to or not. Even if you don't have a Facebook pseudonym or an opposite-gender avatar in Second Life, you are more or less lying every time you say "I" online – because your Facebook actions are always meant to have some kind of limited effect within the context of Facebook, because the formal constraints of the medium and the network greatly limit the "amount" and "quality" of "self" "you" are able to "put" online. Indeed, media have always modulated the "self" of the "artist/author" – painters, writers, dancers, sculptors. [1] Even more radically, philosopher Alfred Korzybski says to use the word "is" at all is a kind of lying, since no single subject could ever be adequately equated to a single predicate. Even more radically, philosophers Gilles Deleuze and Felix Guattari famously undermine the use of the pronoun "I" at all. In the beginning of their seminal *A Thousand Plateaus* they explain:

The two of us wrote Anti-Oedipus together. Since each of us was several, there was already quite a crowd. Here we have made use of

everything that came within range, what was closest as well as farthest away. We have assigned clever pseudonyms to prevent recognition. Why have we kept our own names? Out of habit, purely out of habit. To make ourselves unrecognizable in turn. To render imperceptible, not ourselves, but what makes us act, feel, and think. Also because it's nice to talk like everybody else, to say the sun rises, when everybody knows it's only a manner of speaking. To reach, not the point where one no longer says I, but the point where it is no longer of any importance whether one says I. We are no longer ourselves. Each will know his own. We have been aided, inspired, multiplied. [2]

Obviously, there are some ethical problems with lying. If I am a different "I" from one moment to the next, then the "I" of today no longer needs to take responsibility for the actions of the "I" of yesterday. If the "I" of a conglomerate corporation is protected by certain rights that leave the individual members of that corporation unaccountable for their actions, then we have some problems. But art is not individual citizenship or corporate citizenship. Art is the province of the trickster. Art is always already lying. Ai Weiwei is a trickster artist because the Chinese government is a shifty, lying entity. Even if you're not making overtly political art, materials and media (particularly new media) are lying all the time. Materials aren't even "lying," because that would imply that somehow they were aware of the truth. Materials and media are simply indifferent to our human notions of truth. As anyone who has used or studied color can tell you, colors shift subjectively depending on their context. They fail to remain "true" to their mathematical properties. Art has always already been more about "seems" than "is." Even in the province of science (a famously "is"-y province), "is" can get slippery at very small and very large scales.

There is a famous picture of Yves Klein leaping into the void.

A leap of faith. Then there is a less famous picture of Yves Klein leaping into a safety net. The fact that the famous picture is a lie doesn't really matter. It serves its historical purpose.

The best art liar is David Wilson of the Museum of Jurassic Technology [3]. He is great because he is not really lying. Or better yet, he makes the issue of whether he is or isn't lying less relevant than what he is actually doing, which is something like awaking wonder. And sometimes, in order to do this, he lies.

Recently I got an email from someone who was lying. His fake name is Sebastian Elk. He is trying to find a replacement for himself so he can stop doing whatever it is he is doing. My guess is that he is the webmaster of a wonderful online repository of 20th Century manifestos and periodicals [4] (in the spirit of the original Dada periodical *391*), and he wants someone else to take over his job. Whatever the case, he has now issued two abstract/surreal surveys [5] to help him select his successors. The surveys themselves are wonderful works of lying art.

On the topic of surreal/abstract surveys, here are some more that I really like:

- Jane Dark's Emotion Criteria Exam <www.benmarcus.com/jane_begin.html> (Marcus);
- NODATA <www.slowlydownward.com/NODATA/data_enter2.html> (Donwood/ Radiohead);
- The Will Power Clinic <http://spleen.mcad.edu/spl/clinic/entry.html> (Szyhalski);
- Starfish exams <http://wonderfulscenario.com/exam> (Stanton).

I run a website that may not be lying: http://deepyoung.org. My wife runs a similarly named school that may not be lying: http://

deepyoung.com. My uncle has my same name and he may not be lying: http://curtcloninger.com. Some corny people are fond of saying, "Fiction is a lie that tells the truth." A lie that tells the truth! What a colossal waste of a lie! Why not just tell a lie that tells a lie? Or better yet, why not tell a lie that tells of a speculative future that is not yet and may never become true? [6]

An insane person is not really lying; she just thinks of the truth differently. Maybe artists are insane. If you are an artist on the internet and you aren't intentionally lying, you are really wasting a great opportunity.

///

This essay was originally posted to the *TERMINAL* blog (Austin Peay State University, Clarksville, Tennessee, US). Available online at <www.terminalapsu. org/2013/03/30/on-lying/>.

[1] Cf. Roland Barthes, "The Death of the Author", in *Aspen*, n° 5-6, 1967.
[2] Gilles Deleuze, Félix Guattari, *A Thousand Plateaus*, Continuum Books / University of Minnesota, 2004 (1987). Trans. Brian Massumi, pp. 3-4.
[3] Cf. <http://mjt.org>.
[4] Cf. <www.391.org>.
[5] Cf. <http://4thsearch.wordpress.com and http://4thsearch.wordpress. com/4thsearch-questions-part-two>.
[6] Cf. <http://theyesmen.org/hijinksnewyorktimes>.

2012
Manifesto for a Theory of the "New Aesthetic"

Clement Valla, *Postcards From Google Earth*, 2010 (ongoing). Screenshots from Google Earth, inkjet on paper, 23 x 40 in (58.42 x 101.6 cm).Edition of 5. Courtesy of the artist. Image enacting the uncanny valley. This image is a New Aesthetic image.

Aesthetic experience is always asymmetrical; it needs to be posed in terms of a subject, as well as an object. – Steven Shaviro [1]

What Is the 'New Aesthetic'?

If, according to Guy Debord, "the spectacle is capital accumulated to such a degree that it becomes an image" [2], then the New Aesthetic is technology accumulated to such a degree that it becomes an image. The New Aesthetic (NA) image is a special kind of image – an image which is bodily, affectively sussable by humans. The NA image is not merely (or even) an image to be intellectually pondered by humans. You 'get it' before you understand it (if you ever even come to understand it).

'Things' don't affectively suss the NA image. Only humans 'get it'.

The New Aesthetic is not new (or it has always already been perpetually new). The fact that the NA has recently hit some sort of pop-meme coagulation tipping point (and acquired an ontological name) is merely evidence that technology has finally accumulated to the point of being easily and widely recognised as a collection of Tumblr images without needing to be supported or explained by any underlying theory whatsoever. (Indeed, James Bridle's Tumblr launched the New Aesthetic meme, and Bruce Sterling's journalistic blog dispersed it. [3]) The New Aesthetic has been intuited by hands-on coders for decades (perhaps centuries). It has been discussed by media theorists for at least as long. This is why old school media artists like Mez Breeze and old school media theorists like Simon Biggs (on old school listservs like *NetBehaviour*) are left fairly unimpressed with the current 'gee whiz' enthusiasm about the New Aesthetic. "The future is already here – it's just not very evenly distributed" (William Gibson, in some places as early as 1993 [4]). The future is (always already) in the process of becoming ever more evenly distributed.

When a meme (like 'the New Aesthetic') is initially introduced and received, it is arguably fruitful to leave off theorising about it and avoid trying to codify it. Let speculation and confusion reign and see where things lead. This approach works fine in the beginning; but after a while, it leads to the worst kind of lowest-common-denominator, self-referential, reblogged intellectual sludge.

*The 'New Aesthetic movement' exists only in the imaginations of
a group of bloggers promoting an agenda for which I have no sym-
pathy whatsoever: actor-network theory spiced with pan-psychist me-
taphysics and morsels of process philosophy. I don't believe the internet is an appropriate medium for serious artistic debate; nor do I
believe it is acceptable to try to concoct an artistic movement online
by using blogs to exploit the misguided enthusiasm of impressionable
graduate students. I agree with Deleuze's remark that ultimately the
most basic task of art is to impede stupidity, so I see little artistic merit
in a 'movement' whose most signal achievement thus far is to have
generated an online orgy of stupidity.*
– Ray Brassier [5]

I have taken the liberty of replacing 'speculative realist' with
'New Aesthetic', 'philosophical' with 'artistic', and 'philosophy'
with 'art'.

The New Aesthetic is not a single aesthetic. Drone technology
produces its own visual aesthetics. Google Maps produces its own
visual aesthetics. Generative Processing code produces its own visual aesthetics. Glitches across various media, compression algorithms, and hardware displays produce their own visual aesthetics.
These myriad aesthetics are each as singular and unique as the entangled culture/nature histories which led to the development and
deployment of these various technologies and their gradual accumu-
lation into human-sussable images.

The term 'New Aesthetic' is similar to the term 'New Media'.
When your descriptive adjective is as vague as 'new' (or 'modern'
or 'contemporary'), then all ontological constraints are off. Your
movement is open to embrace 'what's happenin'' in the [future-]
now.

The speculative playing field of the New Aesthetic is even bro-
ader than the speculative playing field of New Media; because

'media' are still indebted to technical, formal, material constraints; whereas aesthetics (even 'old' Kantian aesthetics) have always been philosophically malleable.

Those less theoretically inclined might argue that since the New Aesthetic begins with an affectively intuited image, that's where it should end. Yo Bros, I'm really happy for you. Imma let you finish, but...

The New Aesthetic is not a new flavour of aesthetics. At best, and properly understood, it is a new way of understanding aesthetics altogether, one that renegotiates the relationship between human-subject and non-human-object. Perhaps we need a less historically-encrusted word for this 'new' relationship than 'aesthetic'. But lets keep 'aesthetic' for now. It forces us to revisit Kant, Schiller, Freud, Heidegger, and Whitehead; and those guys had a lot of Tumblr followers back in the day.

"I'm lost in the dark / Lend me your teeth." (Devendra Banhart, 2002 [6]). Post-Media theorist and curator Domenico Quaranta says the New Aesthetic will never be a critical criteria for art unless it grows some theoretical teeth. [7] Currently, it is too preoccupied with surface sheen and not concerned enough with cultural analysis. Agreed. So let's try to grow it some teeth and see what happens...

A Process Without a Singular 'Aesthetic' Intentionality

The New Aesthetic image is like outsider art incidentally created by systems.

The New Aesthetic is indifferent to mimesis. The NA image is not the re-presentation of an object. The NA image is the incidental visual residue of the performance or enactment of a process. The process never intentionally alters itself in order to achieve the 'goal' of the NA image. The NA image is a trace, a remnant, a remainder, a residue, a (potential) clue. The 'subject' of the NA image (when sussed, aright) is the process itself. In this sense, the New Aesthetic is akin to process art, if we substitute 'world' for 'studio' and 'human/non-human entanglements' for 'artist'.

The New Aesthetic image is a Leibnizian 'texture'. It reveals more about the processes and systems that 'produced' it than it does about itself.

Technology was never *evolving toward* the production of this or that NA image. Beware of teleology! Technology was never *trying* to make this or that NA image. Beware of anthropocentrism! (Especially beware of the kind of anthropocentrism committed in the name of overcoming anthropocentrism.)

The difference between Pollock and Cage: Pollock's process is still *heading toward* the production of an aesthetic art object (as judged by his inherited idea of aesthetics). Cage's process is *heading toward* whatever it winds up being. For Cage, chance operations become a vehicle to escape inherited notions of aesthetics. New Aesthetic images are produced by processes that fall somewhere between Pollock and Cage. NA images are not produced solely by randomness, nor are they produced in order to conform to a preconceived human aesthetic. NA images are produced by entangled nature/culture systems. Thus, human will is always partially involved in their production, but it is rarely an aesthetic will *heading toward* the production of NA images. Usually, it is the will to make more money, modulated through complex technological entangle-

ments which have accumulated to such a degree that NA images are incidentally (although not arbitrarily) produced. To fetishise the NA image as a mere 'aesthetic' object is to conveniently ignore the ethical ways in which we are implicit in its production. To fetishistically credit 'machines' as the primary agents behind the production of NA images is to conveniently ignore the ethical ways in which we are implicit in their production.

The New Aesthetic image, in-and-of-itself, *in stasis*, is kind of cool. Cooler yet is the way in which the NA image reveals the historical forces that have come together to 'produce' it in stasis. Coolest is the way in which the NA image reveals how things are currently coming together in process; and how things may possibly come together in the near future.

New Aesthetic images aren't representative, analogous, archetypal, emblematic, or symbolic of any thing else. They are the actual traces and residues of processes and relationships – traces that have arrived in the visual realm and have entered humans via their eyes. NA images don't symbolise or represent the processes that have led to their creation. Instead, they are incidentally thrown into the world by those processes. The way backwards from the images toward the processes themselves is much more complicated that simply intellectually thinking about what these images look 'like'. We initially apperceive NA images bodily and affectively. They are freaky. They trip us out. Only later are we able to reflect on them analytically, letting their own systemic contours and folds guide our theoretical thought.

Because NA images are apperceived and explored along affective lines, submitting these images to pre-existing modes of critical theory (Marxism, feminism, post-humanism, futurist journalism)

may not be enough. What escapes may be more fruitful than what is captured.

Which thinkers are most relevant to the development of a New Aesthetic theory? Deleuze starts to become pragmatically (not just speculatively) relevant. (This might turn out to be 'his century' after all.) Bruno Latour becomes increasingly relevant. Benjamin and Debord remain relevant, but less for their Marxism than their moxie. Baudrillard is a wild goose chase (but then he always was). Graham Harman is a bit of a detour (leading to a dead-end overlooking a noble vista). Whitehead is spot on (but then he always was).

We are not merely left to choose between cyber-utopianism and cyber-dystopianism. Because, like modernism/postmodernism, utopia/dystopia are two sides of the same teleological coin. As Bruno Latour rightly asserts, we have never been modern, we just fooled ourselves into thinking we were. [8] When the truly new emerges, if it is indeed properly new, it won't look like utopia, dystopia, modernism, or postmodernism. It will look (and feel) monstrous and uncanny. "The future can only be anticipated in the form of absolute danger. It is that which breaks absolutely with constituted normality and can only be proclaimed, presented, as a sort of monstrosity."(Derrida, 1967 [9]).

New Aesthetic Images are Affectively Sussed By Humans, Not by Things

An overdub has no choice / an image cannot rejoice
– Carole King, 1968 [10]

It bears repeating: 'Things' don't affectively suss New Aesthe-

tic images. Only humans 'get' NA images. There is no machine 'aesthetic', no robotic 'vision'. Humans invent aesthetic theories regarding the interpretation of machine-generated images. Machines do not invent aesthetic theories regarding the interpretation of circuit-generated images. Likewise, no rock ever invented an ontology. Humans develop ontologies which include rocks. Humans may even philosophically speculate what ontologies rocks might invent. But rocks-themselves do not invent rock-centric ontologies. Nor do rocks-themselves philosophically speculate what ontologies dirt might invent.

If there were a clear dividing line between humans and things, then the 'aesthetics' of the New Aesthetic would lie mostly on the side of humans. Between humans and things, there is no clear dividing line.

The New Aesthetic is not just about intellectually 'getting it' when it comes to technology. Heck, Paul Simon 'gets it' as early as 1986:

The bomb in the baby carriage was wired to the radio... The way the camera follows us in slo-mo. The way we look to us all. The way we look to a distant constellation that's dying in a corner of the sky. These are days of miracle and wonder... And the dead sand falling on the children, the mothers, and the fathers, and the automatic earth... Medicine is magical and magical is art... lasers in the jungle somewhere... Staccato signals of constant information. A loose affiliation of millionaires and billionaires. [11]

Simon's lyric reads like a (much more poetic) version of any number of summative lists recently offered to catalogue the underlying technologies of the New Aesthetic. And that's *Paul Simon in 1986.* Yes, we all get it. We have gotten it for some time now.

The most intriguing thing about the New Aesthetic is that we all now 'get it' affectively via NA *images*. Our human bodies have a way of 'getting it' before our human intellects do.

New Aesthetic images can teach us humans a New Aesthetic. But as we listen to this New Aesthetic, what we are hearing is neither the pure voice of nature nor the *adulterated* voice of machines. We are listening to systems in the world – a world that we are co-creating, a world of which we are always already a part (never apart).

Down With Pan-Psychism!

Pan-psychism is the idea that all things in the world (rocks, animals, predator drones, weather systems, Hello Kitty lunchboxes) have consciousness. The pipe dream of Artificial Intelligence is related to pan-psychism. Pan-psychism is the played-out rabbit trail of the New Aesthetic. "It's a trap!" (Admiral Ackbar [12]). Just because we've finally come to recognise that things and systems have their own agency and are not merely passive and inert, this doesn't mean that things and systems have consciousness.

We humans have become so enamoured of honouring 'the other' that we have come to equate self-denigration with ethical behaviour. Not only do we see ourselves as sexist and racist (which we are), we have come to see ourselves as species-ist (animals are people too) and thing-ist (things are people too). The irony is, as we seek to honour things-in-themselves (thus nobly overcoming our anthropocentric narcissism), we extend to things the highest honour we can imagine – humanness! To imbue things and systems with a kind of consciousness is actually the epitome of anthropocentrism. The conquering European must first dress the native up in civilised clothes before she can be treated as an equal. And now we extend the same ridiculous, narcissistic 'courtesy' to things.

It is not enough that we seek to elevate things to our level; we feel as if we must lower ourselves to thing level. We humans are now no better than things. We are actually mere things ourselves (or mere systems of micro-things, depending on your scalar preferences). And the rocks bow their heads as we pass by, in deference to our enlightened humility.

As a result, we humans are hubristically tempted to attribute the uncanniness of New Aesthetic images to the pan-psychic agency of AI technology. 'Gee, these systems must be sentient (in a way that we humans are sentient), because we humans sure didn't invent these crazy new images.' This response is half-right and all wrong. We humans had a 'hand' in inventing these images, but ours was not the only 'hand'. Systems, materials, things, assemblages co-invented these NA images with us.

Up with Pan-Experientialism!

Pan-experientialism is the idea that all things in the world experience 'being' over time. Forces and events in the world ingress into things in a way that is experienced by those things.

Few things have the same qualitative types of experience. Rock-being-ness isn't human-being-ness (and human-being-ness isn't what it used to be). Alfred North Whitehead puts it like this: experience is the base of all being; consciousness is the apex of all being. So although rocks don't think like humans (indeed, rocks don't think at all), at some base level of being, humans and rocks both experience.

Furthermore, humans don't consciously 'think' everything that we 'experience'. We affectively and bodily experience all sorts of things we don't ever think at all. Only a fraction of our human experiences ingress into our conscious (or even subconscious) awareness.

Pan-experientialism means that humans are a little more like things than we thought, and that things are a little more like humans than we thought. It doesn't mean that humans are mere rocks, or that rocks have consciousness.

We need to understand things as vector forces enacting within networks, not as anthropomorphised objects. Yes, thing have agency, but their agency is altogether thingy. Emergent systems (a.k.a. things made up of things) exercise all sorts of funky agency: flocking behaviours, attraction to strange attractors, radical modulations at state-change thresholds. Yes, non-inert behaviours; but not sentient behaviours. A painter enters into a kind of pragmatic dialogue with the viscous and luminous behaviours of her paint. She need not speculate about its withdrawn essence.

New Aesthetic Images: The Uncanny, the Present-At-Hand, the Sublime

Kansas, I've a feeling we're not in Toto any more
– Dorothy (chopped & screwed)

Aesthetics are related to both experience and consciousness. Aesthetics are born in experience and arrive at consciousness. No consciousness at which to arrive, no aesthetics. So when we talk about aesthetics, we're mostly talking about humans. (Unless we want to radically re-define aesthetics, in which case we should probably use a different word.)

Beginning with Freud: New Aesthetic images are uncanny (*unheimlich*, un-homelike). If NA images were totally familiar, we would read them as family photos. (They are our new family photos.) If they were totally alien, we would read them as so much white noise. Instead, New Aesthetic images are somewhere in-between, in the Uncanny Valley: that disturbing interzone where something 'non-human' is almost human enough to seem 'human', but not quite. We recognise ourselves in NA images, but also something other than ourselves; or rather, still ourselves – but ourselves complicated, enmeshed, othered.

We humans are developing new, more purposefully affective ways of reading these new images.

The only way to read is acrobatically, fast and with lots of background noise (disco music or television), for that encourages more speed and more rapid processing of the information that cannot be processed except as a function of peripheral seeing and distracted absorption… To read poetry carefully and slowly is to miss the point, which is the blur. (Tan Lin [13])

On to Heidegger: Graham Harman interprets Heidegger's *vorhandenheit* (presence-at-hand) as an eruption of the thing out of its normal function in the world (its normal function is *zuhandenheit*, 'readiness-to-hand'). The thing was there all along; but we never saw it this way until now. This eruption is a useful way of understanding NA images. NA images are visual eruptions of everyday functioning systems in the world, systems humans never saw in this way until now. Like Heidegger's broken hammer – the carpenter

only stops to reflect on it once it stops working as expected.

New Aesthetic visuals don't necessarily 'reveal' a hidden 'truth'. It's not as if readiness-to-hand is false and presence-at-hand is true, or vice versa. They are just two simultaneous ways of being in the world. (Heidegger's genius – his 'sleight of hand' – was to draw our attention to readiness-to-hand without turning it into presence-at-hand.)

As per Bruno Latour (and with Heidegger turning in his grave), our current systems have proliferated and hybridised beyond our ken to strange and complex degrees. New Aesthetic images strike at the heart of the modernist myth that man is master and measure of all things. Something much more trippy is actually happening. We are caught up in a proliferation of hybrid hammers ever breaking.

From Heidegger to Kant: New Aesthetic images are more sublime than beautiful. They are sublime because they affectively impact humans in ways which imply the subterranean, ongoing operation of assemblages which have not yet been resolved, and may never resolve; assemblages beyond human mastery, yet in which humans are implicated and entangled. The affective feelings NA images evoke in humans confound Schiller's attempts to reconcile the sensuous and the formal in 'play'. NA images are neither human 'art' nor non-human 'nature'. They were not created to address a static conception of human nature, nor to dialectically overcome preconceived contradictory drives within human nature. Neither were they created by extra-human forces in order to provide human 'subjects' with 'natural' objects for aesthetic contemplation. Instead, NA images are residues that result from current ways of being in the world, entangled ways in which humans are 'always already' implicated. At their best, NA images challenge humans to re-imagine 'humanness', 'being' and 'the world' altogether.

Four Summaries, Three Quotations and a Closing Exhortation

Matter matters. Things (light, networks, economies, rocks, paint, pixels) have their own agency. Things are already in the world, in dialogue with the world, forming and being formed by other things in the world. Indeed, according to Heidegger, things in relationship with other things make up 'the world'. No things; no 'world'. Things don't consciously 'know stuff' about the world, but... things behave in ways derived from their history in the world and from their current entanglements with the world. Things are caught up in the world (of other things), and the world is caught up in things.

'What might things make of the New Aesthetic?' is not a very useful question. 'What might humans make of the New Aesthetic once we realise that we have been entangled with things all along?' is a more useful question. Bruno Latour says that modernism was simply a time when humans thought we weren't entangled with things, when actually we were. What we made of that time unawares was an even bigger entangled mess (Latour's term is 'a proliferation of hybrids') – atom bombs as inverted guardian angels, global warming debates as orthodox scientific catechisms. At this point, it seems unlikely that we are going to avoid further complex human/thing entanglements, so trying to avoid them is probably something we should try to avoid. On the other hand, we should also avoid passively sitting around, techno-fetishistically dazzled by these 'spectacular new developments', blithely watching a real-time documentary of ourselves watching a real-time documentary of ourselves. Probably, we should spend some time figuring out how

these systems flow and function so we can more effectively modulate them (or sabotage them), hopefully for reasons other than making
more money.

All of this stuff is cool. Does it mean that objects have souls, psy-
ches, withdrawn essences, or intelligences? No. Does it mean that
humans are merely one thing among many things, no more or less
endowed with agency? No.

It does mean that humans are recursively entangled with things
and forces in increasingly problematic ways (Bruno Latour told us
this in 1991 [14]). Furthermore, it means that humans affectively
experience all sorts of things in the world prior to (and often without
ever) cognitively becoming aware of these experiences; it means
that things also affectively 'experience' forces in the world; and it
means that systems, ideas, networks, entanglements, forces, events,
technologies, animals, humans and objects are all 'things' in 'the
world'. (Whitehead told us this in 1927. [15] His word for 'things'
is 'entities.') The fact that a bunch of people are currently talking
about all this stuff online simply means that our technology has accumulated to such a degree that it has become an image – an image
we can all (tech geeks, object oriented philosophers, sci-fi journa-
lists, tumblr-ing graphic designers, twenty-something net.artists,
rocks) affectively suss.

*

"I have no doubt that in reality the future will be vastly more surprising than anything I can imagine. Now my own suspicion is that the Universe is not only queerer than we suppose, but queerer than we can suppose." (J. B. S. Haldane, 1927 [16]).

"There is no need to fear or hope, but only to look for new weapons." (Gilles Deleuze, 1990 [17]).

"Be very very quiet / Clock everything you see / Little things might matter later / At the start of the end of history." (Steely Dan, 2003 [18]).

*

Do carry on funking & wagging, but with rigour. Little things might matter later.

///

This essay was originally published in *Mute Magazine* (London), online and in print. Available online at <www.metamute.org/editorial/articles/manifesto-theory-'new-aesthetic'>

[1] Steven Shaviro, "The Universe of Things," *Theory And Event 14*, no. 3 (2011): 16.
[2] Guy Debord, *Society of the Spectacle* (Detroit: Black & Red, 1983), Part 1, Note 34.
[3] James Bridle's Tumblr can be accessed here: < http://new-aesthetic.tumblr.com/>. Bruce Sterling posted his "An Essay on the New Aesthetic" on *Beyond the Beyond*, his blog on Wired.com, on April 2, 2012. The essay is still available at <www.wired.com/2012/04/an-essay-on-the-new-aesthetic/>.
[4] For more on the gradual historical distribution of this quote, see: <http://quoteinvestigator.com/2012/01/24/future-has-arrived>.
[5] Modified from Ray Brassier , "I am a nihilist because I still believe in truth," interviewed by Marcin Rychter (Lebanon, February 2011), *Kronos* (4 March 2011), URL: <http://kronos.org.pl/index.php?23151,896>.

[6] Devendra Banhart, lyrics from "Lend Me Your Teeth," *Oh Me Oh My by Devendra Banhart* (New York: Young God Records, 2002).
[7] Domenico Quaranta, "Una Nuova Estetica?", *Flash Art 303* (June 2012): 26.
[8] Cf. Bruno Latour, *We Have Never Been Modern* (Cambridge, Mass: Harvard University Press, 1993).
[9] Jacques Derrida, *Of Grammatology* (Baltimore: Johns Hopkins University Press, 1976), 5.
[10] Carole King, lyrics from "The Porpoise Song," *Head by The Monkees* (Culver City, California: Colgems Records, 1968).
[11] Paul Simon, lyrics from "The Boy in the Bubble," *Graceland by Paul Simon* (Burbank, California: Warner Bros. Records, 1986).
[12] *Star Wars Episode VI: Return of the Jedi*, prod. Howard Kazanjian, dir. Richard Marquand, 136 min., Lucasfilm, 1983.
[13] Tan Lin, "Anachronistic Modernism," *Cabinet Magazine 1* (2000/2001), <http://cabinetmagazine.org/issues/1/anachronistic.php>.
[14] In Bruno Latour 1993, cit.
[15] In Alfred North Whitehead, *Process and Reality: An Essay in Cosmology* (New York: Free Press, 1978).
[16] J. B. S. Haldane, *Possible Worlds and Other Papers* (New York: Harper & Brothers, 1928), 286.
[17] Gilles Deleuze, "Postscript on the Societies of Control," *OCTOBER 59*, (Winter 1992), 3-7, <www.n5m.org/n5m2/media/texts/deleuze.htm>.
[18] Walter Becker and Donald Fagen, lyrics from "GodWhacker," *Everything Must Go by Steely Dan* (Burbank, California: Reprise Records, 2003).

2011
Bergson's
"Spirit"

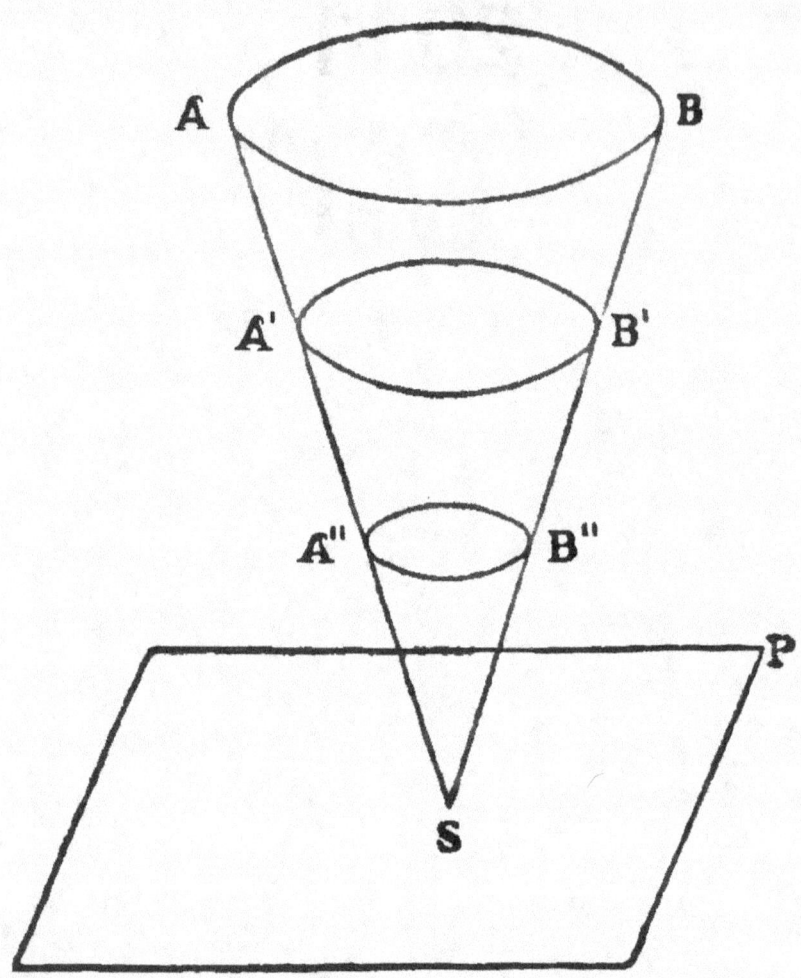

Figure 3 from chapter III of Henri Bergson's *Matter & Memory*, "the authorized translation" by Nancy Margaret Paul and William Scott Palmer, published in 1912 as part of the "Muirhead Library of Philosophy" series by G. Allen & Unwin Company of London. In the diagram, the present is depicted as an isometric plane which intersects an inverted cone of memory.

Henri Bergson's understanding of time, memory, matter, and the mind has gone in and out of academic favor, largely depending on the latest discoveries in neuroscience. But to read Bergson as a kind of amateur Victorian neuroscientist, crippled by the science and technology of his time, is to miss the potential revolutionary thought of Bergson's philosophy. [1]

Radically, Bergson proposes a space (which is not a space or place at all) that he calls "spirit." Bergson's spirit is not necessarily the Judeo-Christian "spirit" mentioned in the Bible, and it is certainly not the loose, subjective "spirit" of most contemporary new age forms of spirituality. [2] Bergson's spirit is related to memory, and it is specifically and directly contingent upon the ways in which humans encounter matter in the world. Bergson rejects the idea that the brain is like a hard drive which stores memories. If our memories are not stored "on" a hard drive some*where*, then our memories have more to do with time than with space. They are never translated into a binary some*thing* and stored in a physical somewhere. Time is never directly reducible to space.

If our memories aren't stored "in" our brains, then "where" are they stored? Even this question reveals how difficult it is for language to avoid thinking in terms of Cartesian space. Bergson says that our memories aren't any*where*; our memories are spirit – they have occurred in historical time, and they are accessible by us at any given time. Bergson comes very close to proposing that all our memories, from the earliest to the most recent, are accessible by us in the present.

The reason we don't have instant and total recall of all these memories is that such total recall would flood us with an overwhelming tide of recollections, feelings, and options, rendering us unable to function in the present. So our memories are effectively filtered by the matter surrounding our bodies in the present. If a large rabid dog is running toward me very fast, baring its fangs and growling, I will rapidly access any memories I have of being pierced by sharp objects or knocked down by rapidly approaching large objects. These recalled memories are then experienced by my body in the present as a kind of affective force that colors and informs my present actions. This filtering process isn't limited to situations of extreme danger. The sound waves of music, the smell of perfume, the feeling of being crowded by bodies in a subway car – every present tense situation in which my body encounters matter prompts me to access, filter, and parse spirit/memory. To Bergson, dreams are simply the open, refracting connections that memory makes when it is not filtered and constrained by exposure to present tense matter in the world. [3]

There are a number of exciting implications to Bergson's philosophy of time. First, according to Bergson's system, humans have agency in the world. We are not limited to materialist, behavioralist responses. There is an immaterial realm of memory/spirit that may be accessed and invoked in order to color and modulate our present tense behavior in the material world. Furthermore, this spiritual realm is not binarily severed from the material world. It is contingent on the present tense, historical/material world. Likewise, the present tense, historical/material world is contingent upon this spiritual world of memory. Matter and Memory. Memory and spirit are thus "real." Bergson's "spirit" is not "scientific" per se, but neither is it "religious." It might best be understood as "philosophical," but this by no means makes it merely theoretical or unreal.

A second implication of Bergson's system is that memory compounds and folds back on itself. I initially remember, and then later I am able to both remember and to remember myself having remembered. Every time I revisit a Polaroid picture of my childhood, I remember my childhood differently, in an increasingly compounded manner. I can begin to feel nostalgic for the way nostalgia used to feel. Thus memory is not a static archive; it is a living, changing, ongoing series of real-time events.

A third implication of Bergson's system is that memory always eventually comes back into the present through some form of human action on matter in the world. Even contemplative thought can be a form of present action, if it eventually leads to any kind of making or doing – writing, art, social action, interpersonal affection, etc. Michel de Certeau's concept of "tactical" living begins to gain greater agency in this light. No form of matter (and media is matter) is ever passively encountered or "consumed." As I watch television, as I read, as I surf the internet, I "make do" (de Certeau's term) – I make my way through my encounter with this matter, making of it what I will; and this matter/media in turn invokes memories that color/inflect my present actions. [4]

For example, let's say I read a Facebook post by a friend, perhaps a quotation from Proust. This quotation leads me through a series of thoughts, memories, ideas, and emotions that will eventually enter the present in the form of some sort of action. [5] This is not to say that every single exposure to matter always invokes a profound chain of memories inevitably leading to an epic, historically significant action. Some resultant actions matter a lot; other actions matter less. But all actions matter to some degree. And since all actions are invoked by matter in the world, matter in the world necessarily "matters." In the final sentence of *Matter and Memory*, Bergson

succinctly summarizes this mutually contingent relationship betwe-
en matter and memory/spirit:

*"Spirit borrows from matter the perceptions on which it feeds, and
restores them to matter in the form of movements which it has stamped
with its own freedom." [6]*

Matter and memory (spirit) are not separate, nor is one subordi-
nate to the other (as if our memories were stored as data on physical wetware; or conversely, as if the entire material world were a
mere "spiritual" illusion). The two realms are intrinsically contingent upon one another. This contingency becomes important from a
pragmatic perspective. One critique of Hakim Bey's famous "Temporary Autonomous Zone" concept is that it only changes one's own
subjective mental state. The T.A.Z. doesn't really change the material world. But if one's own mental state is intrinsically contingent
upon the material world, and if one's own mental state directly (or
indirectly) influences the present-tense, material/historical world,
then suddenly "changing one's mind" might not be so subjectively ineffectual after all. Indeed, although early internet utopianists
latched onto Bey's "T.A.Z." essay as one of their core philosophical
documents, Bey himself writes in that same essay that unless the internet can deliver exotic materials and services (illegal "food, drugs,
sex, tax evasion") to his physical door in the present, then he doubts
its efficacy. [7]

So the things I read and watch, the order and manner in which
I read and watch, the way I move my body through the world – all
of these things begin to matter. There is no longer a dualistic divide
between matter and memory (spirit). Once I am aware that matter

affects memory affects matter, I can begin to purposefully modify and modulate this affective cycle. Instead of simply exerting all of my energy against matter with the assumption that "the spiritual" doesn't exist (or that it is effectively severed from / irrelevant to "the material"), I can purposefully employ spirit (memory) in my attempts to modulate matter. Sometimes my experiments will have little effect. Sometimes they will have great effect. A rigorous experimental practice is required. [8]

The fourth (and final) implication of Bergson's philosophy of time involves an original model of "the real." Bergson's "real" (as taken up by Gilles Deleuze) divides into two realms – "the virtual" and "the actual." None of this has anything to do with "Virtual Reality" (data gloves, headsets, avatars, 3D environments). Bergson's "actual" real describes all of the forces that have come together in the confluence of historical time to form what we know as history. The actual is that aspect of the real that has been historically actualized. The actual has "come to pass" historically, and we know it now as "the past." The actual can only ever be actualized in the present, and then it immediately passes into history – it becomes that which has happened.

The "virtual" real is comprised of all those forces surrounding the present, awaiting actualization in the confluence of historical time. The virtual is comprised of those forces which have not yet coalesced in time. These forces may coalesce in time in a billion different possible combinations, and/or they may never coalesce in time at all. The virtual is still "real," because it is contingent on actual history thus far. The virtual is not comprised of every single force that may ever exist at all times. It is not an abstract, imaginary, or hypothetical realm. In short, the virtual is not "unreal." [9]

So, for example, in the early 1940s, prior to the historical actualization of the atomic bomb, the contingent forces necessary to bring the atomic bomb into existence were all in place (technically, materially, culturally, politically, scientifically). From this perspective, in 1940, the atomic bomb was an aspect of the virtual real. Whereas in the 1400s, the atomic bomb was not a part of the virtual realm, because the contingent forces necessary to bring it into historical existence were not yet in place. In the 1400s, the atomic bomb was unreal – both actually and virtually.

The virtual is not merely "potential" or "possibility," because the possible is already glimpsed from within the actual. As soon as I am able to recognize in the present historical moment the "possibility" of something coming into being, then it has already become actual. Now it simply awaits implementation. So, for example, digital computing arguably becomes "actual" (from a Bergsonian perspective) in the 1800s when Charles Babbage conceives his plans for the Difference Engine, prior to any implementation of the machine itself. [10] The virtual is that which could coalesce historically in the present moment, but which has not yet been actualized (or even conceived as possible).

The development of this "actual/virtual" model of the real is attributed to all sorts of folks (Bergson, Marcel Proust, Alfred North Whitehead, Gilles Deleuze, and Brian Massumi, to name a few). Although Deleuze is the one who most thoroughly formulated and articulated this model of the real, I find it there in Bergson at least as early as 1896. [11] Deleuze takes up Bergson's model of the real and makes of it a kind of pragmatic ethic for both "experimental" art and "speculative" philosophy. If the virtual is not mere potential, but is "actually" unknown (unknown to the actual), then how might an artist or a philosopher develop a rigorous method of actualizing the virtual? By definition, whatever this method looks like, it cannot be based on known outcomes (because it is trying to trick something into being that is heretofore unknown). Nor can it be merely a method of hybridizing two actual things into a third actual thing. It must be a method of bringing something into being – not *ex nihilo*, not from "the void," but from a real virtual realm that is contingent upon all of history up to the present moment.

Deleuze's experimental ethic is progressive by definition ("progressive" as opposed to "conservative"). Any method of actualizing the virtual may wind up actualizing something horrible and monstrous, something much worse than that which has already been actualized. [12] The degree to which one finds the status quo unacceptable is the degree to which one might risk practicing Deleuze's experimental ethic. Once you believe, "Anything is better than this," then you are ready to begin the dangerous practice of actualizing the virtual.

As it turns out, actualizing the virtual is not as dangerous as it seems, because the virtual is not all that easy to purposefully actualize (at least not to any degree that makes much pragmatic difference). Furthermore, any attempt (artistic and/or philosophical) to actualize the virtual is inherently open to accusations of impracticality, irrationality, ineffectuality, and speculation. [13] These accusations will always be inescapable, at least until the virtual has been actualized and new criteria have emerged within the actual by which to judge the pragmatic efficacy of any recently practiced experimental approaches. Even then, these newly emerged criteria will be powerless to immediately assess the efficacy of the next wave of actualizings. None of this is an excuse to experiment non-rigorously and willy-

nilly, but it does suggest that any criticism based on actual/historical criteria (and what other kind of criticism could there be?) be deferred until all the results are in. Thus, Deleuze's entire speculative project of purposefully actualizing the virtual is always performed as a kind of ongoing ethical wager.

In reality, the virtual is being actualized all the time. The actualization of the virtual is simply known as "history coming to pass." [14] What makes Deleuze's project different is that it calls for a purposeful actualization of the virtual based on a novel Bergsonian understanding of "the real" – an understanding derived not from an analysis of things which have already come into being, but from a model of the process of "coming-into-being" itself.

Despite its inherent weaknesses, Bergson's model of the real has much to offer the pragmatic agitator. It proposes at least one method for opening up a space of human agency in the present. As developed by Deleuze, Bergson's model leads to a speculative, artistic/philosophical practice that functions like a machine for causing things to emerge. Art and philosophy are no longer tools for analyzing and mimetically imitating "actual" things that have already historically emerged. We transition from tools for analysis to machines for advancement, from analytical assertions to speculative wagers. [15] These tactical transitions are all based upon and made possible by Bergson's understanding of memory as "spirit."

///

This essay was originally published in *Nictoglobe's Friction Research 4 - Reclaim The Mind* (The Netherlands). Available online at <http://nictoglobe.com/new/query10.html?d=rtmfr42011&f=cloninger_on_bergson>.

[1] In this essay, I will limit my reading of Bergson to his first two books, *Time and Free Will* (1889) and *Matter and Memory* (1896).

[2] Perhaps Bergson should have chosen a less historically laden/loaded, less blatantly un-scientific term than "spirit" (Deleuze's "plane of immanence?" Heidegger's "being-in-the-world?") Or perhaps "spirit" is the perfect word to blatantly challenge overtly materialist explanations of the mechanics of memory.

[3] The following Mickey Newbury country music lyric seems relevant: "My world is like a river as dark as it is deep / Night after night the past slips in and gathers all my sleep / My days are just an endless stream of emptiness to me / Filled only by the fleeting moments of her memories / Sweet memories // She slipped into the silence of my dreams last night / Wandering from room to room turning on each light / Her laughter spills like water from the river to the sea / And I'm swept away from sadness clinging to her memories / Sweet memories". From the song "Sweet Memories", 1968.

[4] The difference between mediated matter vs. "real" matter is the linchpin of all media theory. I would argue that a stone and a video of a stone are both real and material; but in radically, qualitatively different ways (which I won't attempt to unpack in this footnote). There is a Marxist thread running through media theory that passes from Hegel to Marx to Walter Benjamin to Guy Debord to Jean Baudrillard, a thread which might be summed up in Marx's famous dictum, "All that is solid melts into air." Furthermore, much has been written on the difference between the way a stone activates memory vs. the way a video of a stone activates memory. Paul Virilio's insights on speed seem particularly relevant to the ways in which mediated matter affect human memory and action.

[5] Bergson actually understood thinking in the present as its own kind of legitimate historical action.

[6] Henri Bergson, *Matter and Memory*, trans. Nancy Margaret Paul and William Scott Palmer (London: G. Allen & Co, 1912), final page.

[7] "Let's say that for both political and personal reasons I desire good food, better than I can obtain from Capitalism – unpolluted food still blessed with strong and natural flavors. To complicate the game imagine that the food I crave is illegal – raw milk perhaps, or the exquisite Cuban fruit mamey, which cannot be imported fresh

into the U.S. because its seed is hallucinogenic (or so I'm told). I am not a farmer. Let's pretend I'm an importer of rare perfumes and aphrodisiacs, and sharpen the play by assuming most of my stock is also illegal. Or maybe I only want to trade word processing services for organic turnips, but refuse to report the transaction to the IRS (as required by law, believe it or not). Or maybe I want to meet other humans for consensual but illegal acts of mutual pleasure (this has actually been tried, but all the hard-sex BBSs have been busted – and what use is an underground with lousy security?). In short, assume that I'm fed up with mere information, the ghost in the machine. According to you, computers should already be quite capable of facilitating my desires for food, drugs, sex, tax evasion. So what's the matter? Why isn't it happening?" - Hakim Bey, *T. A. Z. The Temporary Autonomous Zone, Ontological Anarchy, Poetic Terrorism*, Autonomedia, New York 1985, 1991. Available online at <http://hermetic.com/bey/taz_cont.html>. Quoted from Part 3, the section entitled "The Net and The Web."

[8] A call to this kind of rigor is implicit in the following passage. Here, Bergson is not calling for a mere theoretical, abstract, ideated "knowing." He is calling for a kind of rigorous, actual, material/historical, embodied knowing: "It is one thing to understand a difficult movement, another to be able to carry it out. To understand it, we need only to realize in it what is essential, just enough to distinguish it from all other possible movements. But to be able to carry it out, we must besides have brought our body to understand it. Now, the logic of the body admits of no tacit implications. It demands that all the constituent parts of the movement shall be set forth one by one, and then put together again. Here a complete analysis is necessary, in which no detail is neglected, and an actual synthesis, in which nothing is curtailed." Henri Bergson, *Matter and Memory*, Chapter II, 139.

[9] Marcel Proust's description of that which is constant in both the past and the present serves as a succinct definition of "the virtual" (and is frequently quoted by Deleuze to describe such): "real without being actual, ideal without being abstract." Marcel Proust, *In Search of Lost Time*, Set, vol. 6, *Time Regained* (New York: Random House Pub. Group, 2003), 264.

[10] This is not to say that implementation is irrelevant. I am simply illustrating the difference between the possible and the virtual.

[11] Chronologically, Proust began writing *In Search of Lost Time* over fifteen years after Bergson completed *Matter & Memory*, but this hardly proves Bergson's influence on Proust's thinking. Bergson was married to Proust's cousin, and Bergson and Proust corresponded with each other; but there is some evidence that Proust was not directly influenced by Bergson's philosophical theories. Deleuze and Whitehead both openly acknowledge their debt to Bergson, and Massumi his debt to Deleuze.

[12] Jacques Derrida observes: "The future can only be anticipated in the form of absolute danger. It is that which breaks absolutely with constituted normality and can only be proclaimed, presented, as a sort of monstrosity." Jacques Derrida, *Of Grammatology*, trans. Gayatri Chakravorty Spivak (Baltimore: Johns Hopkins University Press, 1997), 5.

[13] Philosophy and art have been inherently open to accusations of impracticality, irrationality, ineffectuality, and speculation for millennia, so perhaps they are the perfect vehicles for Deleuze's experimental project.

[14] As Keanu Reeves banally observes in *Bill & Ted's Excellent Adventure* (Stephen Herek 1989), "The world is full of history."

[15] The British philosopher/mathematicians Bertrand Russell and Alfred North Whitehead famously collaborated on *Principia Mathematica* before going their separate philosophical ways. Russell subsequently pursued analytic philosophy, whereas Whitehead pursued a path more akin to speculative (continental) philosophy. Tellingly, Russell has significant problems with Bergson's philosophy, whereas Whitehead admires and expands upon it.

2010
GltchLnguistx: The Machine in the Ghost / Static Trapped in Mouths

The image of happiness from Chris Marker's *Sans Soleil* (France 1982, color, 100 m. Directed by Chris Marker, produced by Anatole Dauman for Argos). Screenshot taken from Youtube excerpt of the movie.

This essay applies Mikhail Bakhtin's language theory of "the utterance" to the machinic event of "the glitch" in order to illuminate contemporary glitch art practices, and to suggest fruitful ways in which they might proceed. I understand "the glitch" to be an affective event generated by a media machine (computer, projector, game console, LCD screen, etc.) running in real-time, an event which creates an artifact that colors and modulates any "signal" or "content" being sent via that machine. In 1962, John Glenn famously defined "glitch" as "a spike or change in voltage in an electrical current." [1] "Glitch" has since come to demarcate a set of audio/visual artistic practices which capture, exploit, and produce glitch artifacts.

My goal is not to end all conversation about glitch art by ontologically overdetermining what a glitch is and how exactly it works. Instead, I pose this specific, particular position in the hopes of ending some of the more dead-end and circular conversations about the glitch. I also hope this essay will open up more fruitfully problematic conversations, and will lead to less banal, more conceptually rigorous works of art.

Dichotomies To Be Exploded

It is a cliché of early cyber-theory to embrace the transcendental ideal of disembodied code and run with it. According to this approach, humans are simply data run on wetware. If we could somehow abstract this data and port it to computer hardware, we could upload our souls/selves. We could become the ghost (disembodied spirit/ code) in the machine (computer hardware). This hope of disembodied immortality is rooted in some specious, idealistic presuppositions about the way computers and humans actually work. Much of "who" humans "are" is inextricably bound to the action of our bodies in lived and present time. Likewise, computers don't execute code in a transcendent, metaphysical vacuum. Code is run on physical hardware in lived and present (albeit massively accelerated) time. Computer code (like human language) may theoretically exist in a timeless transcendental realm, but in order for it to intersect being, it has to be read by and run on something – a person or a computer. The glitch foregrounds and problematizes this myth of pure transcendental data, of pure and perfect signal. The glitch is a perpetual reminder of the immanent, real-time embodiment of executed code.

The myth that humans can upload their souls is related to the myth of pure signal transference. Both of these myths are derived from residual Platonic dichotomies which need to be exploded. Some of these Platonic dichotomies are:

immanent / *transcendent*
physical / *metaphysical*
body / *spirit*
hardware / *software*
incarnation / *disembodiment*
in time / *out of time*
lived life / *philosophical ideals*
uttered event / *language system*
emotion/volition / *content/meaning*
present event / *memory*
glitch event / *glitch artifact/trace*
compiled and running code / *source code*

These dichotomies are not binary opposites. They are not even gradual continua transitioning slowly from one extreme to the other. Instead, these extremes are inextricably enmeshed. Furthermore, they are not simply enmeshed (like the contours of an infinity symbol, evenly phasing back and forth between extremes). No, they are much more complicatedly, erratically, and problematically enmeshed (like an abstract diagram of Deleuzean relationships). [2] Furthermore, they are not haphazardly, randomly, or aleatorically enmeshed. No, they are rigorously, fine-grainedly, contingently enmeshed. These extremes intersect and entangle in the ongoing, lived and present moment. This ongoing, lived and present moment is the moment of the glitch and the moment of the utterance.

Signals About Signals (A Controlled Experiment)

One way to test what a system is doing is to send human language through it and see what happens. Human language is complex. It involves a transcendent, linguistic system (as Noam Chomsky observes). It also involves semiotic play of meaning (as Jacques Derrida observes). But (as Mikhail Bakhtin observes), human language ultimately involves real-time, affective utterances – speech acts based on individual human will (volition) that occur in a specific lived context (time and space, here and now). So human language is both transcendent and immanent. It foregrounds the strange/complex intersection of these two purported extremes (metaphysical/out of time vs. immanent/in time). What happens to human language when it is glitched by media machines? As receiving humans, we still try to semiotically decode such language (language as a system of "meaning"), but we also experience it as a material, affective force (language as utterance/event).

Some instructive instances of language sent down a glitch-laden path are not necessarily from the glitch art community. One example is from a live concert video of Peter Gabriel's song "Secret World." A video of Gabriel's face is projected onto the surface of water. He begins talking about underground disturbances that gradually irrupt and manifest themselves as surface disturbances. As he talks, the water onto which his face is projected shakes increasingly, destabilizing the image of his face. The media machine here is very analog – the mirrored surface of water. [3] A similarly analog (though more hardware-driven) example occurs in the famous video of Dan Sandin demonstrating his *Analog Image Processor*. The live video

of Sandin's demonstration is fed through the machine itself in real time. As we watch a video of Sandin's hand turning a knob, that knob modulates the video we are watching of his hand turning the knob. The more he turns the knob, the more the image of his hand turning the knob is qualitatively affected.

Philosophers as Adhesives

Perhaps philosophers are like adhesives. You have to pick the right one for the job, and there is no single right one for every job. Plato is like Elmer's Glue: he is ubiquitous; he holds things together well enough; and everyone has swallowed him at a young age unawares without any immediately fatal results. Derrida is like duct tape: it is tempting to apply him to everything, but if you apply him too liberally to problems that need a less than all-encompassing approach, the results will be very sticky and munged-up with a bunch of deconstructive residue which largely obscures the original problem. If Marshall McLuhan is a thin rubber band (more or less useful in his analysis of media), then Guy Debord is a thick rubber band (trying earnestly to outwit the trap of media spectacularization), and Jean Baudrillard is a silly band (resigned to play in a mediated simulacrum).

Of course these are oversimplifications, but not necessarily unuseful ones. The philosophers from which you launch will necessarily color the subsequent inquiry of your art theory and practice. In order to analyze the glitch, I've chosen Russian philosopher and literary theorist Mikhail Bakhtin. [4] Bakhtin is like gaffer's tape. He adheres tightly when suitably applied, but he releases his grip

quickly when it is time to decouple things and move on to new lo-
cales and configurations.

Bakhtin and The Utterance

Before I oversimplistically explicate Bakhtin's theory of the utterance, I will begin with some direct quotations:

*Language enters life through concrete utterances (which manifest lan-
guage) and life enters language through concrete utterances as well.
The utterance is an exceptionally important node of problems.* [5]

*Only the contact between the language meaning and the concrete rea-
lity that takes place in the utterance can create the spark of expression.
It exists neither in the system of language nor in the objective reality
surrounding us. Thus, emotion, evaluation, and expression are foreign
to the word of language and are born only in the process of its live
usage in a concrete utterance.* [6]

*Each text (both oral and written) includes a significant number of va-
rious kinds of natural aspects devoid of signification... but which are
still taken into account (deterioration of manuscript, poor diction, and
so forth). There are not nor can there be any pure texts. In each text,
moreover, there are a number of aspects that can be called technical
(the technical side of graphics, pronunciation, and so forth).* [7]

To Bakhtin, the lived and ongoing present is the locus where the
abstract rules of linguistics and semiotics are injected into being.
Language never comes into the present generically. It is always colored by and contingent upon embodied, contextual affects of lived being. I can say "I'm hungry" at a certain place and time, and
someone else can say "I'm hungry" at a later place in time. Both
sentences are linguistically and semiotically the same, but they are

completely different "utterances" due to the differing lived contexts into which they were uttered.

Unlike Derrida, Bakhtin satisfactorily takes into account the importance of embodied affect on human language. The breeze blowing through my wife's hair as she meets me in the yard and says, "Welcome home, honey," the timbre in her voice, the tilt of her head, the angle of the sunlight striking her cheek – all of these things are as much a part of human language as the denotative/semiotic meaning of the English word "welcome." [8]

Bakhtin is particularly useful for analyzing the glitch because he doesn't overtly fret over the differences between a "live" event and a "mediated, time-shifted" event. When I read a book in real-time, that reading event constitutes a live utterance, because the author of the book is uttering to me in lived time now. The typography of the book, the way the cover feels in my hands, the way the light falls on the page of the book – all of these are real-time, embodied affects that color the language of the book in the same way that the breeze through my wife's hair colored the language ("welcome") she uttered when she met me in the yard. The language of a book on a shelf may be transcendental and out of time, but that language will never get "run" in real-time unless I open the book and read it. When I do, embodied affect enters into the flow of language and colors it in an actual, "meaningful," non-incidental way.

Modulating Language via Affect

The first scene of Chris Marker's *Sans Soleil* celebrates the surplus of lived, embodied affect. A scene of three blond-haired girls walking on a road is shown briefly. The scene doesn't semiotically or linguistically "mean" anything, which may be why the film maker (the fictitious sender of letters to the narrator) is unable to successfully couple the scene with any other images. The film maker associates this surplus of affect with both memory and happiness. [9]

In my own new media reinterpretation of Marker's scene [10], I associate this surplus of affect with the history of photography, the disturbing uncanniness of dreams, and the glitch. It is worth noting that the particular low-resolution video file I used is a much degraded and massaged version of a DVD quality version of Marker's original analog film. Yet even the original analog film is not a record of the film maker's original lived experience on that day. Derrida becomes useful here (briefly, but fundamentally): there is always a slippage, an original difference between something in itself (the girls, the fence, the hills) and our perception of it. All subsequent meaning in language derives from this original difference.

According to this understanding of affect, glitch, utterance, and original difference, everything is "always already" mediated. Debord wants to return to an original, real, unmediated experience. Baudrillard says we can no longer return to that original real experience, because we have moved beyond mimetic mediation and on into simulation and hyper-reality. The problem with both of these positions is that "media" are (and always have been) "real." Language spoken in a movie playing in real-time is language actually uttered in real-time. Granted, it is a strange kind of second-order language, a quoted and remixed language (what Bakhtin might call a "secondary genre" of utterance, like characters speaking in a novel), but it is no less a real-time, uttered language event. A book, a video, a piece of software – all contain potential utterances. Each piece of media awaits its next real-time run when it is uttered into a unique, singular, never repeatable, spatio-temporal, lived context.

A glitch is like the wind blowing through a speaker's hair. A glitch injects lived affect into the live utterance. Glitches arises from the immanent "world." (According to Heidegger, "the world" consists of things connected to other things within being.) Of course, once we digitize and increasingly "mediate" our human language, then the coughing, sputtering, extra-semiotic forces of the world can more readily (and radically/rootedly) modulate our language, at increasingly deeper and more fine-grained structural levels. The static of the world gets trapped in our mouths.

Note, however, that glitched language is never merely pure affect, because it always retains a residue (however violently glitched) of semiotic meaning and linguistic structure. There is always a non-affective element of language riding the waves of glitched affect; or, conversely, there is always a non-affective element of language that glitched affect is able to surf. McLuhan was hyperbolic to say, "The medium is the message." Actually, "medium | message" wind up being just one more Platonic dichotomy awaiting explosion and rigorous entanglement.

The Machine Accelerates Lived Time/Space Affects

The glitch event is not "unnatural." It's just that we humans are still acclimating ourselves to it. We are less used to seamlessly absorbing it as affect. Analog affect is more qualitatively gradual, whereas digital affect can dramatically spike. This explains the difference between warm analog overdrive distortion [11] and the binary disconnect of digital overdrive distortion. The quality of analog distortion is related to the nature of its source signal, whereas digital distortion is simply a complete miss – one second you are hearing the source signal, and the next you are hearing a monotone beep.

The digital visual glitch can have a similarly jarring effect. When I come home to the "welcome" of my wife, the breeze may increase slightly through her hair as she is speaking, and I subtly perceive and absorb this gradual affective modulation. Were she to somehow digitally glitch, it would be as if the wind increased to hurricane force in an instant, and then in the next instant it was back to a light breeze. Such is the thrilling violence of the digital glitch. It can be so jarring that we simply filter it out as so much noise and refuse to even perceive it.

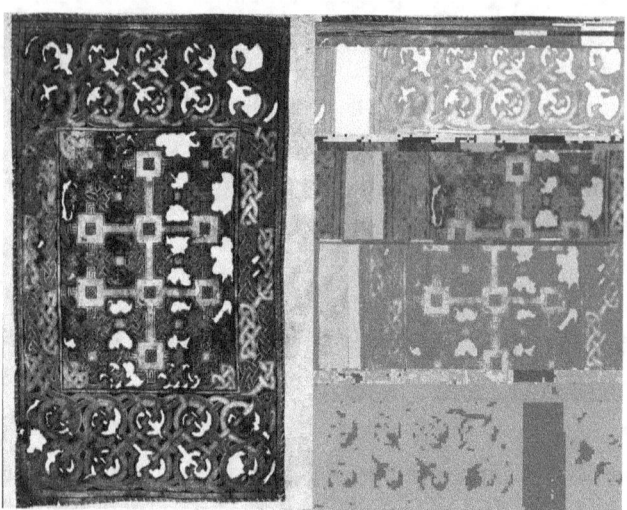

Left: the *Book of Durrow*; right: a digital glitch of the *Book of Durrow* jpg achieved by corrupting the file's source code in a text editor.

The *Book of Durrow* is a (very) old school analog glitch. It is a piece of analog "media" created around 680 A.D. which has gradually glitched over the last several hundred years. Certain parts of it were colored with a pigment that has eaten away at its vellum substrate. This glitch actually follows the contours of the original ornamentation. It is a very slow glitch.

Unlike pigment and parchment, the computer is like a space/time accelerator. An analog page may wrinkle or fade, but a computer screen constantly refreshes (60-80 times per second). The computer is perpetually "doing;" it is always "performing" in real-time. So it throws off affective anomalies more frequently (quantitatively) and more extremely (qualitatively). Digital glitches are thus more instantaneous and frequent, but they also follows specific formal contours of decay. Different compression codexes glitch in different formal ways.

Wild vs. Domesticated Glitches

A glitch is actually an affective event that happens in time. The results of such a glitch may be captured (by taking a screen shot of the visuals produced during a glitch event). This captured glitch may be thought of as the trace of a glitch, the residue of a glitch, or the archive of a glitch. These glitch traces may be thought of as "wild glitches." [12]

Glitches can also be intentionally produced by artists trying to achieve a purposeful glitch effect. Glitch artist/theorist Rosa Menkman calls these intentional glitches "domesticated glitches." [13] The term "glitch art" might apply to all domesticated glitches and all wild glitches that have been "captured" and recontextualized as art.

Thus far I have mostly been examining the phenomenon of "wild glitches," but my observations are equally applicable to "domesticated glitches," because both glitches ultimately and finally "run" not on computers, but on human wetware in real-time. Both glitches are experienced by humans as a spike or a surplus of affect.

Are there particular sub-genres of domesticated glitches? Free range, organic, grain-fed, etc. (software mods, hardware mods, file corruption, etc.). Different glitch mod(ification) tech(nologie)s do indeed have different affects. These affects extend beyond merely different "visual aesthetics." These different modifications are actually bodily experienced in qualitative different ways, including but not limited to the recognition of visual forms. A rigorous and exhaustive taxonomy of glitches might be interesting, but it would prove very difficult (just as Bakhtin's call for a rigorous taxonomy of various speech genres has never fully been answered). Casual speech genres and technological glitches are constantly evolving, because social human situations and hardware/software technologies are constantly evolving.

Politics of the Determination of Signal vs. Noise

There is a brief moment in the cyberpunk film Johnny Mnemonic where a TV news broadcast in the lobby of a posh hotel is temporarily interrupted by a glitchy "pirate signal" of a patchworked face saying, "Snatch back your brain, zombie. Snatch it back and hold it." A bellhop and the titular character (played by Keanu Reeves) briefly focus on the hijacked broadcast, but once the regular news broadcast returns (the announcer says, "Sorry, technical difficulty"), they immediately forget the interruption as if it had never occurred. In this dystopian future, noise (as opposed to signal) has become so prevalent, political dissent is conveniently filtered out as a mere technical glitch.

I want to reflect on the "political" implications of the glitch. (According to Bruno Latour, "politics" are simply shared matters of human concern that congregate around things in the world). Lived affects color lived utterance. As such, lived affects matter. But they can also be filtered out by those seeking a pure transcendent "signal." As "listeners," we learn to negotiate increasing amounts of "mediated interference." We are always trying to cognitively filter "noise," trying to find our way back to a "natural/real" state of normal. But this return to "natural normal" is impossible. It's not impossible in a Baudrillardian sense (there is no real, only simulation). It is impossible precisely because "mediated simulation" has always already been "real." Mediated language is "real" language. It has "real" affect which "really" inflects and colors its "real" semiotic meaning.

The attempt to regulate and filter out irruptive "noise" and return to the ideal of a pure signal is the same metaphysical/Platonic attempt to downplay the immanent and maintain (the myth of) the pure transcendent. Subverting (literally "deconstructing," in Derrida's original sense) this dichotomous, binary metaphysical system is a radical (root level) "political" act.

As humans, we can increasingly marginalize "the other" until we no longer consider them "other." Emmanuel Lévinas's ethics derive from the face of the other, but if I erase the face of the other, if the other is sub-human, if the other receives no body count when I am adding up my casualties of war, if the other is merely vague collateral damage, then I am no longer ethically obliged to even respect them as "other." They are treated as noise to be filtered. Genocide as ethnic filtering.

Rosa Menkman begins to apply Foucault's ideas on "madness" to the topic of signal vs. noise. [14] I would like to expand on the implications of this application. If I define your signal as "wrong," I have already entered into dialogue with it. I have recognized your signal as admissible; we simply disagree. But if I define your signal as "madness" or "noise," then your position no longer demands an ethical answer of me.

Academics may filter out non-academically validated positions as noise. Believers may filter out non-faith-based positions as noise. Radicals may filter out non-radical positions as noise. Moderates may filter out non-moderate positions as noise. The list is endless. Such filtering keeps us from having to individually assess and respect the overwhelming number of voices and positions clamoring for our attention. But filtering noise is never "politically" neutral; it always involves an initial and sweeping value assessment which then excuses us from having to make subsequent, case-by-case value assessments based on specific individual positions.

It is one thing to personally and willfully filter a source signal as noise. It is a much more problematic thing to have that noise filtered out for you unawares. Certain consumer electronic devices filter out user agency by offering a very limited number of pre-set options. There seem to be at least two critical artistic approaches to such pre-set noise filtering: 1) cynically revel in these pre-sets, call attention to them, use them to make art that ironically celebrates them, and claim that the failure of your art is an intentional foregrounding of the failure of pre-set culture. 2) hot-wire your pre-set devices and force them to do glitched-out things they were never meant to do.

The second approach seems more promising in the long run, if for no other reason than that it risks advancing something. What seems like liminal noise might wind up being the very (diagonal) line of deterritorialization that leads to a better, emergent, heretofore unimagined future. Ancient Greek philosophy introduced the idea of the clinamen, a minute swerve in the flow of falling atoms that caused a chain reaction which led to variety, agency, and emergence in the world. Without this swerve, there was no change. Perhaps the glitch is such a swerve.

The general ethical challenge becomes: Do I maintain my current understanding of what it is to be human by perpetually filtering out, staving off, and defending myself from the "noise" of the glitch event in order to perpetuate the myth of a pure signal; or do I welcome the noise of the glitch as "natural" and learn to lean into it? In order to embrace the glitch as something other than noise to be filtered, I will have to risk modifying my own signal/noise ratio – this will entail modifying my "aesthetics" and my human "self."

One final note regarding the purported impotence of art as mere "symbolism." Glitch art is not merely "symbolic" of a politics of noise tolerance. If language is affective and mediated, if politics are shared matters of human concern that congregate around things in the world, then glitch art doesn't merely "symbolize" a political stance; it actively practices one. Could the glitch become a mere aesthetic fad? Could glitch artists become glitch Nazis, growing increasingly less tolerant of non-glitch signals? Yes, of course. All these things have already happened. Still, the fact that something can be fetishized and commodified is hardly grounds for its categorical dismissal (since everything, even Marxist theory, can and has been fetishized and commodified).

Some Strategies

Here are some pragmatic strategies for the practicing glitch artist. Hopefully they will lead to more engaged, relevant, rigorous, fun, messed-up work.

Invite The Immanent In

When you create, don't hard-bake your glitch media. In other words, don't find a glitch, isolate it, and then send it down the line as a perfect glitch specimen (encased in digital amber). Instead, open up your transfer mechanisms to subsequent glitch events. As a net artist, I prefer animated gifs and layered xhtml/css [15] rather than the controlled/baked environment of Flash. The speed of animated gifs (with frame delay set to 0 seconds) is determined by the speed of the user's local processor. CSS and XHTML invite other platform-specific and browser-specific anomalies. Resizing the browser window yields different formal compositions. Separate elements of the page load at different rates depending on the speed of the user's internet connection. All of these technical considerations invite the immanent event into the art.

Bakhtin's comments on painting seem particularly relevant in this regard:

Finalized, or "closed" individuals in painting (including portraiture)... present man exhaustively; he is already completely there and cannot become other. The faces of people who have already said everything, who have already died [or] may as well have died. The artist concentrates his attention on the finalizing, defining, closing features. We see all of him and expect nothing more (or different). He cannot be reborn, rejuvenated, or transformed – this is his finalizing (ultimate and final) stage. [16]

It is instructive to compare the figures in Giotto's *Raising of Lazarus* (1305) to the figure in Gerhard Richter's *Woman Descending the Staircase* (1965). Giotto is the master of the solid, self-contained, hermetically sealed human subject. The humans in his

paintings look like discrete, separate objects. Richter is the master of the dissipated (and dissipating) human subject. When Richter's paintings are reproduced digitally, his glitch effects seem baked in, but this is only because the source medium of the snapshot is being returned to itself in the form of the digital thumbnail. Live and in person, Richter's actual paintings are an entirely different event. Walking toward and away from his canvases invites the immanent glitch event into the viewing experience at every distance. Entire paintings seem to dissolve at close proximity.

Glitch Your Own Criteria of Glitch Reception

There are two main categories – signal vs. noise. Signal has two sub-categories: signals that matter vs. signals that don't. Likewise, noise also has two sub-categories: glitches that are worth pursing/ keeping/archiving/posting/claiming vs. glitches that get edited/ignored/not captured. The glitch artist and the "wild glitch" collector are their own curators at every turn – deciding which outcomes to keep and which to ignore; but...

1. Based on what criteria? Based on marvel, surprise, authenticity (unstaged-ness [related to surprise]), messed-up-ness, kitschy retro-ness, "beauty," promise/fruitfulness (a potential to lead somewhere new)?

2. How can we glitch our own criteria of glitch reception? How can we glitch ourselves so that we don't always select the same old glitches? Cagean aleatoric systems? Oulipian systems of constraint? Collaborative systems?

Warning: there are some inherent problems when glitching your own "aesthetic" criteria. At some point you are going to have to fall back on meta-criteria in order to determine whether your newly glitched aesthetics are aesthetically successful. It is a bit like shooting at a moving target, like using drugs and then trying to objectively evaluate the effect of the drugs while you are still on drugs.

Recognize That Humans Are the Last Mile of Runtime

Regardless of what analog or digital systems you use to massage your glitch, it still ultimately has to "run" on human wetware. Could you develop a system or make a work of art that causes human wetware itself to glitch? Tony Conrad's flicker films, Brion Gysin's dream machine, and Op Art all seem applicable. Glitching language is a promising place to start, because the semiotic aspects of language always run in real-time on human wetware in tandem with (and inextricably entangled with) the embodied, affective aspects of your glitch.

///

This essay was originally presented at the First Annual GLI.TC/H Noise and New Media festival in Chicago and published in the book *GLI.TC/H! READER[ROR] 20111* (Tokyo: Unsorted Books). Available online at <http://lab404.com/glitch/>.

[1] John Glenn, cited in *American Heritage Dictionary*, 4th ed. (2000), s.v. "glitch"; quoted in Iman Moradi, *Glitch Aesthetics*, (B.A. diss., The University of Huddersfield, 2004), 9.
[2] For fun, cf: Marc Ngui's wonderfully ridiculous illustrations of Deleuze & Guattari's *A Thousand Plateaus*, available online at <www.bumblenut.com/drawing/art/plateaus/index.shtml>.
[3] On the topic of water as a reflective medium, it may be worth noting that McLuhan claims Narcissus did not fall in love with "himself," but with his own mediated image. cf: Marshall McLuhan, *Understanding Media; The Extensions of Man* (New York: McGraw-Hill, 1964), Chapter 4.
[4] I am primarily drawing from three texts: Bakhtin's early (mid-1920s) essay fragment published as *Toward a Philosophy of the Act* [trans. Vadim Liapunov (Austin: University of Texas Press, 1993)]; His 1953 essay "The Problem of Speech Genres;" and a series of 1971 notes published as "The Problem of the Text in Linguistics, Philology, and the Human Sciences: An Experiment in Philosophical Analysis."
[5] Mikhail Bakhtin, "The Problem of Speech Genres," in *Speech Genres and Other Late Essays*, trans. Vern W. McGee (Austin: University of Texas Press, 1986), 63.
6Ibid., 87.
[7] Mikhail Bakhtin, "The Problem of the Text in Linguistics, Philology, and the Human Sciences: An Experiment in Philosophical Analysis," in *Speech Genres*, 105.
[8] Cf. The Seals & Crofts lyric "Summer Breeze" for a wonderfully sappy, idealized celebration of pure affect.
[9] The narrator's words from the famous opening scene of *Sans Soleil*: "The first image he told me about was of three children on a road in Iceland, in 1965. He said that for him it was the image of happiness and also that he had tried several times to link it to other images, but it never worked. He wrote me: one day I'll have to put it all alone at the beginning of a film with a long piece of black leader; if they don't see happiness in the picture, at least they'll see the black."
[10] Check it out at <http://playdamage.org/76.html>.
[11] Cf. David Bowie's production of The Stooges' "Search and Destroy."
[12] Visual glitch theorist Iman Moradi uses the term "pure glitch" to describe what I am calling "wild glitch." Cf. Moradi, *Glitch Aesthetics*, 8-11.

[13] Rosa Menkman, "Glitch Studies Manifesto," (Amsterdam/Cologne: 2009/2010), 7. Moradi uses the term "glitch-alike" to describe what Menkman calls "domesticated glitches."
[14] Ibid., 11.
[15] For reference, check out <http://playdamage.org>.
[16] Bakhtin, "The Problem of the Text," 115.

2009

Commodify Your Consumption: Tactical Surfing / Wakes of Resistance

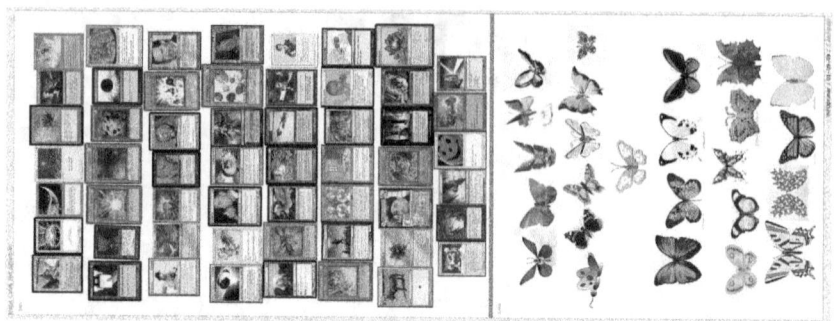

Magic Cards and Butterflies (screenshot, rotated counter-clockwise). Posted by INFOpruner on *Spirit Surfers* in September 2009 <http://www.spiritsurfers.net/monastery/?p=887>

Applying a theory to a practice not only illuminates the practice; it opens up new ways of understanding the theory. Here I want to apply Michel de Certeau's seminal text *The Practice of Everyday Life* to the contemporary practice of "artistic surfing" in the hopes of broadening an understanding of both. What I'm calling "artistic surfing" (aka "surf clubbing," "spirit surfing") takes its inspiration from group blogging, particularly anonymous group photoblogs like 4chan.org. Internet "surf clubs" are basically invitation-only group photoblogs where artists surf the internet intuitively and obliquely, collect detritus (predominantly from commercial sites and social networking sites), recontextualize it via bricolage, titling, and Photoshop remixing, and post it at the surf club's blog where it is often further recontextualized and reposted. [1]

The Practice of Everyday Life proves very useful in analyzing this mode of artistic surfing. Internet surfing is basically a hybrid of reading and walking, both practices that *The Practice of Everyday Life* explores in detail. In order to properly apply de Certeau to artistic surfing, I will have to recoup him (or at least borrow him)

88

from the cadre of "tactical media" artists and theorists who have claimed him as their patron saint since 1997. [2] In the process of my analysis, I will propose a gradual continuum between production and consumption, discuss the differences between "deep" net art and "surface" net art, pragmatically redefine "resistance," and explore some ways that tactical consumption might be intensified in order to efficaciously modulate the network and the world.

A Production / Consumption Continuum

In 1980 de Certeau observed that academics analyzed media either in terms of its content ("information") or in terms of its delivery mechanisms ("television" in his era, "networks" in our era). What was lacking was a way to talk about the creative "reception/consumption/use" happening at the consumer end of the line – how were the "users/consumers" modulating institutional input in the practice of their lives? They weren't merely passive receivers. In de Certeau's words, "To assume that [the public is moulded by the products imposed on it] is to misunderstand the act of 'consumption.' This misunderstanding assumes that 'assimilating' necessarily means 'becoming similar to' what one absorbs, and not 'making something similar' to what one is, making it one's own, appropriating or reappropriating it." [3]

De Certeau described an implicit dichotomy between production and consumption. On the production side were strategic institutions who had power, financial resources, and an established physical base of operations. On the consumption side were tactical users/consumers who lacked power but were more mobile than institutions. "A tactic is determined by the absence of power just as a strategy is organized by the postulation of power." [4]

Into the midst of this dichotomy, the web introduces a problematic entity – the hobbyist user. The hobbyist user (aka prosumer, surfer, social networked netizen) doesn't have the productive agency of an institutional corporation, but she has more productive agency than de Certeau's original television viewer. She can't produce Hollywood movies, but she can upload YouTube videos.

As early as 2000, Nicolas Bourriaud wrote, "There is (fertile) static on the borders between consumption and production that can be perceived well beyond the borders of art." [5] Four years later Nato Thompson argued,

The dependence on these two terms [strategies vs. tactics] seems to create a barren but much needed middle ground. Instead of a polarizing dichotomy, maybe it would be more useful to consider these terms as the two poles of resistant aesthetics. That is to say that a project vacillates in its relationship to power from tactics to strategies. While owning the dominant system may feel impossible, it feels more than a little slackerish to depend on defeat. [6]

I here take up their challenge and pose a cursory continuum, ranging from strategic production to tactical consumption.

1. Producer (tied to "spatial or institutional location", production of physical objects) [abstract expressionist artist as hero]
2. Protester (opposes corporate production, but in a way that produces its own form of spectacle) [overtly "political" '70s art]
3. "Tactical Media" Artist (ephemeral actions, but still ends up in galleries and art history books) [Critical Art Ensemble]

4. Remix Artist (perpetually remixes media as a talisman against being commodified) [D.J. Spooky]

5. Artistic Web Surfer (reconstitutes found source material as the trace of a surfed path through the web) [surf clubs, MySpace video remixers, 4chan users, "filter feeder" link list curators] [7]

6. Theorist (poaches source material from language and remixes it in the form of ideas, attributes sources in order to give props and leave bread crumbs) [Talmudic commentators, scholarly researchers, Deleuze creating new "ideas" from Spinozan and Nietzschean source material]

7. Anarchist Drifter (purposefully wanders in order to reconstitute space, often just for herself) [Hakim Bey's "Temporary Autonomous Zone," Debord's derive, Baudelaire's flaneur]

8. de Certeauian User/Consumer (watches television, reads books, walks around, and personally reconstitutes the meaning of the one-to-many streams of media broadcast at her) [all humans who watch, read, walk, cook, and live; the majority of whom are not artists.]

Note that, according to this continuum, artistic surfers are actually operating closer to what de Certeau originally means by "tactical use" than many "tactical media" artists are. This is because "tactical media" artists have never really been "consumers." By and large they use de Certeau's analysis of writing and walking (and cooking and living) as a kind of metaphor for more overt forms of subversive action (denial of service attacks on hardware or genetic mutations of wetware). In conjunction with the art institutions that feature such "tactical media" work, these actions can be considered (admittedly weak) forms of institutional strategic production. Whereas artistic web surfers are actually reading and wandering (they let their fingers to the drifting, so to speak).

De Certeau's analysis of reading fits naturally when applied to practices of artistic surfing:

"[Consumers are] unrecognized producers, poets of their own affairs, trailblazers in the jungles of functionalist rationality... They trace 'indeterminate trajectories' that are apparently meaningless, since they do not cohere with the constructed, written, and prefabricated space through which they move." [8]

Replace "consumer" with "artistic web surfer" and the sentence seems as if it were written in 2008.

This weaker tactical position is neither inherently better or inherently worse (it's better in some ways and worse in others). My point is that the dichotomy between strategic production and tactical consumption is more fruitfully understood as a continuum with middle ground.

Institutional Production of the "Interactive Subject"

The problem is, not all forms of web 2.0 "interactivity" are inherently "tactical." Put another way, mere "use" does not automatically constitute "resistance."

Is using off-the-shelf corporate software to create a "unique/personal" MySpace page a way of subverting the institutions of mass media production, or is it simply one more example of these institutions using the myth of "originality" to assimilate and amass a demographic market of "unique" individuals? Artists who use these templates have to be particularly wily if they hope to keep from being assimilated and rendered "tactically" impotent.

How do you hack/resist a platform that already allows (indeed, invites) you to customize it? Either we have arrived at an open source utopia and we simply need to keep using these social networking tools appreciatively in the ways that they afford; or the agency of our radical "resistance" has been rendered irrelevant because the corporations have decided to let the people eat cake (provided we eat their particular brand of interactive cake).

The agency that de Certeau's consumer enacted to tactically reassemble the one-to-many media broadcasted to her in 1980 is being increasingly usurped by institutionally recommended (and protocologically enforced) modes of interactive behavior. Once the consumer mistakes these institutional "suggestions" for the exercises of her own tactical agency, she fails to exercise that actual agency. With so many "customizable options" available, how can she "resist?" [9]

In a fleeting moment of insight, Billy Joel sings, "I got remote control and a color TV / I don't change channels so they must change me." The corollary may actually be more accurate. [10] The more I change channels, the more they change me. I sacrifice my "resistant" agency at the altar of trivial difference. The danger of MySpace and YouTube is not the threat that they may wind up archiving and owning all the "content" I produce, or that they are currently getting rich off the content I produce, but that they control the parameters within which I produce "my original" content.

"Production" turns out to be an amorphous term. It begs the question "production of what?" Now that "consumers" have become "content producers," we should be asking ourselves, Who are the

meta-producers? Who produces the contexts surrounding "creative" prosumer production? Who produces the tools that suggest the proper "way" in which amateur's are to produce? These meta-producers are no longer producing "content." Or rather, their "content" is the production of an "interactive" human subject – a subject who feels autonomous, empowered, and creative; but who may have difficulty enacting any pragmatic agency. This transition from spectacularized consumption to spectacularized production is insidious.

The placebo effect of web 2.0 "empowerment" is at least as problematic as the original one-to-many TV effect of disenfranchisement. At least in 1980 there was a suspicion that something needed to be resisted.

Deep Net Art and Surface Net Art

I want to propose another continuum that is related to the production/consumption continuum, but not an exact mirror of it. Deep net art is net art made by programmers/coders/hackers who attempt to modulate the network by opening up its hood and tweaking it down toward its protocological core. Surface net art is net art made by artistic net surfers who attempt to modulate the network by staying on the surface of the network and tweaking in amongst the images, animations, videos, human languages, and other readymade media that travel across its surface. [11]

In 1990, Gilles Deleuze wrote that "societies of control operate with... computers, whose passive danger is jamming and whose active one is piracy or the introduction of viruses." [12] According to this model, surface net art can be considered a kind of passive culture jamming that occurs at the level of uttered human language, and deep net art can be understood as the active viral piracy that occurs at a machine code level.

In general, early net artists were more concerned with code than contemporary net artists are (this is an oversimplification). [13] Contemporary net artists have a lot of online tools, templates, and content already developed for them, so they can afford to be less concerned with code and content production. YouTube and MySpace aren't radical in their underlying architecture; they are radical in their mass popularity and ease of use. [14]

Compare an earlier net art piece like Mark Napier's *Shredder* [15] with a contemporary net art piece like Oliver Laric's *50 50*. [16] Both pieces "remix" online media, but Napier's remix happens at a deep level. He's under the hood of the browser itself (although not exactly at the level of TCP/IP network routers). Laric's piece happens at a surface level. It's really a video piece. It need not be viewed online. It qualifies as net art simply because it takes its content from YouTube and conceptually examines YouTube culture. It is art "about" net culture.

When I say "deep" and "surface," I don't mean that one is better and the other worse. I'm just describing a level of technical engagement. Both of the above pieces are conceptual, and both pieces are formal. By engaging at a deep level, Napier's piece conceptually problematizes the myth of "form vs. content." By engaging at a surface level, Laric's piece conceptually problematizes the myth of "unique identity via subculture participation." The concepts are different, and the formal aesthetics are different; but that doesn't mean that one piece is completely conceptual and the other piece is completely formal. Different methods of artistic production lead to different conceptual and aesthetic outcomes.

The Wake: Strong Consumption as Weak Production

"Once the images broadcast by television and the time spent in front of the TV set have been analyzed, it remains to be asked what the consumer makes of these images and during these hours." - *Michel de Certeau [17]*

Unlike watching television, artistic surfing literally makes something out of time spent surfing (whether link lists, found object bricolage galleries, or surface modulated media). These traces or "wakes" [18] are then turned back out onto the web for others to see. In this sense, artistic web surfing is like reading on steroids – it is a kind of reading that leaves a trace which can itself be read. Even prior to "artistic surfing," a browser's history retained a wake of the surfer's movements through the web. This wake could be exported as an HTML document and posted back onto the web. [19] Delicious bookmarking simply makes such wake externalization easier, taxonomical, and more user-curated. Surf clubs like Spirit Surfers exercise an even stronger form of consumption. Surfers post not only their "wakes" (bread crumbs and field notes from their surfing excursions in the form of relevant source material), but also their "boons" (remixed and/or recontextualized "booty" – found digital objects, conceptual tropes, and bricolaged nuggets that are the "product" of such surfing excursions). This form of strong consumption (artistic web surfing) results in forms of weak production (a surf club post, a YouTube remix, a delicious bookmark list).

This externalization of the artist's internal, subjective derive modulates the existing web dataspace. The web (or at least those micro-

cosmic sections of the web located at surf club URLs and delicious. com) is modulated from an undigested, pre-surfed commercial space into a newly modified, post-surfed, modulated space – a space that has been put to "tactical use." Technically, artistic web surfing is hardly a radical practice. Anybody posting a link from their weblog is "technically" doing almost the same thing. The "art" of this practice is in qualitative meme modulation rather than deep level technical skills. As with academic research, success depends on the particular sources you choose and the ways in which you choose to contextualize them – creation via selection, compilation, and enframing.

Enacting a Way, Not Producing an Object

The associative connections we make between the discrete pieces of media we receive every day exert a kind of "in-between" agency. Internalized, these associative connections contextualize and thus control a large portion of our personal experience. Externalized and distributed (commodified), they may begin to exert a similar liminal agency, one less co-optable by institutions. These associative connections are not merely autonomous, idiosyncratic, and subjective. Instead, they negotiate an ongoing equilibrium between received media form and exerted consumer will. Like tightrope walking, these associative connections enact and maintain a perpetually negotiated balance of meaning within a system that includes the tightrope walker herself as part of the equation. |20| These thinking, reading, surfing, poaching, associative connections operate as de Certeauian tactics.

Ultimately, the "products" of artistic surfing are not simply discrete pieces of media. Instead, any instantiated results are best understood as traces or wakes produced by the movement of the artist over the surface of the web. These enacted wakes may then begin to resonate sympathetically with other surfers moving along the web surface in similar ways. These externalized associative connections transmit tactics of becoming to those who have ears to hear, transmissions that are difficult to decipher by the corporate radar. These externalized wakes produce something not so much "resistant" as simply alterior. They enact and celebrate the joy of surfing itself, of making connections, of thinking at all.

Here again, de Certeau's description of the act of reading is readily applicable to the act of artistic surfing. He says that reading consists of all sorts of "detours, drifts across the page, metamorphoses and anamorphoses of the text produced by the travelling eye, imaginary or meditative flights taking off from a few words, overlapping of spaces on the military organized surfaces of the text, and ephemeral dances." [21]

In his watershed 1945 article "As We May Think," Vannevar Bush envisioned a personal computer capable of constructing "memex paths." [22] These paths were trails that a researcher took through data, with particular associative connections permanently archived and taxonomized by the researcher. Its contemporary equivalent might be a something like a wiki or ShiftSpace where the researcher can add her own hyperlinked associations between discrete pieces of data, meta-tag these associations, and then save the entire thread/derive/wake/path. [23] Bush prophetically envisioned that these paths could then be linked by the researcher to other related paths, and that these meta-webs of micro-paths could be shared

with other researchers. I could link into your memex paths and you could link into mine. As Ted Nelson has lamented, thus far the web has only realized a fraction of Bush's more robust vision for memex path functionality.

In the context of artistic surfing, Bush is important because he introduces the concept that a kind of knowledge can be transferred from one person to another (or from the same person to herself years later) not simply by aggregating discrete content, but by exteriorizing the paths that a person takes through discrete content. Bush's proposed memex paths are a kind of enacted, vectorial knowing – a knowing that modulates through and is modulated by "content," but that is itself "contentless" and not synonymous with content. Think of surf club threads as Dadaist memex paths on lo-res absinthe.

Rag & Bone

"Can't you hear us yelling 'rag and bone'? / Bring out your junk and we'll give it a home / A broken trumpet or a telephone / C'mon and give it to me" – White Stripes

Associative connections are impossible to make without some form of source content to connect, and the content of most artistic surfing is surface web junk. This is not to say that artistic surfing is about junk, but that it is enacted on/in/through junk. Artistic surfers begin with (apparently) banal visual content so that any clever visual pun or trope they make seems all the more clever, because the subject matter itself is so (apparently) crappy. This move (selecting and modulating junk) foregrounds ways of reading rather than what is being read.

Selecting corporate detritus (along with banal, prosumer/hobbyist detritus) foregrounds the spaces in between the content rather than the content itself, but it also has a particular embodied affect, since all matter (even a badly animated gif) matters. I will take a cue from Kevin Bewersdorf [24] and compare surf clubs to Joseph Cornell's boxes, but in order to reveal differences rather than similarities. Cornell's boxes are simultaneously melancholy and wondrous because they extract objects from their used, embodied, immanent, material, historical contexts and suspend them in an idiosyncratic, museological ether. Cornell's boxes reveal and enshroud the historical project of the enlightenment gone melancholically awry. Whereas surf club posts expose a kind of modernist cultural amnesia – a perpetual, blanking reset where thing after thing after thing is endlessly culled from the churning corporate well of an eternal now[here]. Unlike Cornell's boxes, the "objects" bricolaged in surf club posts are immaterial, appropriated not from the corner antique store, but from the corporate ether. As a result, I find a lot of surf club "work" not so much pathos-inducing as "pathetic" (and not necessarily in a derogatory sense). It feels kind of like gleeful children making absurd sculptures out of strewn body parts in a land-mined field that they have always known, a field inherited from a war they can't remember. All very post-Dada. If Cornell's work enacts the slippages of memory; then artistic surfing enacts the manic, doomed attempt to manufacture any kind of memory at all in the fluorescent light of an eternally modern present.

This fetishistic fascination with junk has its promising aspects and its dangerous pitfalls. When done well, this kind of surfing plunges into the stream of corporate detritus, inflecting and modulating it from within (it tactically enacts and externalizes ways of

connecting). When done poorly, this kind of surfing lapses into a kind of banal wallowing whose wakes are no more transformative than the original detritus through which they move (it simply becomes about a fetishistic love of junk). As George Santayana wryly observes, "Americans love junk; it's not the junk that bothers me, it's the love." [25]

The "resistant political value" of well-done artistic surfing is that it enacts, externalizes, and virally propagates a "tactical" way of moving through corporate culture. As I read these externalized readings (surf club threads, YouTube remixes), I don't just read "about" their source content, or even "about" how they operate; I am compelled (or at least invited) to "re-enact" their operation – to read them in the same way they themselves have read. To poach de Certeau, "[These practices] say exactly what they do. They constitute an act which they intend to mean." [26]

Things Speaking To Each Other

"A tactic boldly juxtaposes diverse elements in order suddenly to produce a flash shedding a different light on the language of a place and to strike the hearer." - Michel de Certeau [27]

Artistic surfing, like conceptual art and stand-up comedy, relies on placing just the right elements in just the right context with just the right inflection at just the right time. It is an art of economy. In this respect, the analog patron saint of artistic surfing may not be Duchamp in his readymade phase (since he was dealing with discrete singular objects in the context of institutional critique), or Joseph Cornell (since he was dealing with

memory and the archive), but Haim Steinbach and his curious object ensembles.

Steinbach claims that objects "have functions for us that are not unlike language." [28] Unlike the object ensembles of Fred Wilson or Mark Dion, Steinbach's objects are not stand-in signifiers for abstract signifieds (colonialism, consumption, New England history, etc.). Instead, because of the strangely purposeful/purposefully strange way Steinbach selects, arranges, displays, and labels them, his objects begin to resonate with each other (to "speak to" each other) in a way that implies a disontological syntax of embodied sympathies. This syntax has something to do with the physical characteristics of the objects (color, surface material, weight, reflectivity) and something to do with their cultural history (what they are actually used for, what era they connote), but it is not simply a composite of these two components. In some sense, their syntax happens in addition to them. This implicit disontological syntax is also governed by the way the objects are positionally in the world in relation to each other. Steinbach's rigorously constructed shelves and their precise placement on the wall are as much a part of his work as the objects themselves. Fellow sculptor Lisa Lapinski argues, "The shelf works are fractions: the things in the world divided by the minimalist object." [29]

All objects in the world are probably related to each other in a similar way, but we humans aren't used to perceiving these irreducible relationships (and the objects themselves feel no obligation to disclose them to our ontological "minds"). The genius of Steinbach's installations is that they begin to hint at this mysterious embodied syntax that might exist amongst all objects. Whether and in what form this syntax of objects actually exists is ultimately unverifiable, but the mere suggestion of its existence is disontologically thrilling. Art critic Bruce Hainey succinctly and poetically summarizes Steinbach's work: "Wittgenstein begins Philosophical Investigations by quoting Augustine's *Confessions* on the naming of objects. Steinbach pulls his quotations directly from the world; his confessions deranged in glorious 3-D approach the unnameable." [30]

Although "found" online "objects" are immaterial, their forms can be serialized and juxtaposed so that they take on a sculptural quality. Like Steinbach's physical objects, these immaterial "things" also begin speaking to each other. Such dialogue is not surprising. Language may be "immaterial," but it is still an immanent force in the world (like electricity or gravity).

At its best, surf club bricolage is more than merely a series of inside jokes amongst a select group of net.junk aficionados, but something more akin to the minimal conceptualism (or conceptual minimalism) of Steinbach.

The "art" of such ensembles is largely in their enframing. Here again, de Certeau is applicable: "This [tactical] response is singular. Within the ensemble in which it occurs, it is merely one more detail – an action, a word – so well-placed as to reverse the situation." [31] The discrete "things" themselves will never look like much. They are by definition unspectacular. This is why their enframing has to be particularly deft and clever.

Resistance Is Futile (or How I Learned To Stop Kicking Against The Pricks)

"There is no need to fear or hope, but only to look for new weapons."
- Gilles Deleuze [32]

Whenever anyone starts playfully remixing corporate junk, the ethical question inevitably arises, "How is such work resistant?" This question implicitly accuses the work of one or more cardinal sins: pragmatic impotence, "political" disengagement, intellectual wankery, regressive formalism, "personal" inauthenticity, and getting duped by the institutional strategies that all artwork is obliged to "resist." (Jeffrey Nealon argues that "Resistance implies or necessitates a kind of totalized, normative, repressive enemy and/or a kind of authenticity of subversive response." [33]) The easy answer to this challenge is a familiar one: "This art is not political." But if (following Bruno Latour) we define politics as matters of public concern that gather around "things" (rivers, bridges, weather systems, laboratory equipment, buildings, food, networks, images, and yes, even pixels), then all art work is inherently political.

Rather than simply dodge the question, "How is artistic surfing resistant?", I want to question the implicit assumption that resistance is always the best tool for the job.

Resistance is Reactionary

By definition, one problem with resistance is that it is reactionary. As institutional strategies shift from the production of objects to the production of "interactive subjects," resistance is forced to shift inversely. Eventually, institutions begin to anticipate these resistant reactions and incorporate them into their proactive strategies. Rather than playing this incessant game of cat and mouse with the corporations, why not choose a "proactive" political goal not defined by negation?

Resistance Is Already Everywhere

"Power is nothing other than what it does." – Jeffrey Nealon [34]

"Life-resistance is nothing more than the act of living."
– Alex Galloway and Eugene Thacker [35]

Another problem with the idea of "resistance" in and of itself as a radical art move is that resistance is already everywhere. Domination and resistance are both forms of power, and power is always omnipresent. [36] Jeffrey Nealon asks, "Resistance to what... We can hardly position ourselves 'against' power, wealth, and truth itself in any kind of wholesale way insofar as any kind of effective critique will have to work toward redeploying those very resources of power, truth and/or wealth." [37] Likewise, Geert Lovink asks,

Is it possible for tactical media makers, activists and artists... to take an amoral position and see control as an environment one can navigate through instead of merely condemn it as a tool in the hands of authorities? [38]

By definition, anyone web surfing (or reading, walking, cooking, living) is already "resisting" (in some form, however weak) imposed institutional strategies of production. In *The Practice of Everyday Life*, de Certeau doesn't radically call for resistant forms of tactical consumption to be invented from scratch. Instead, he radically illuminates how forms of tactical consumption have always existed.

Resistance Is Dead. Long Live the Emergent Virtual.

Henri Bergson's concept of "the virtual" continues to supersede the concept of "political resistance" as a contemporary ethical goal of artistic production (at least in those circles where artists still feel the need to maintain some sort of ethical goal). If the goal of "political resistance" is to stick it to the man, then the goal of "the emergent virtual" might be to modulate and inflect both ourselves and "the man" until these binary dichotomies are tweaked into something heretofore unknown (beyond mere dialectical resolution or synthetic hybridization, since those two things are already known). This "heretofore unknown" is what Bergson calls "the virtual." Will the virtual be better or worse than where we are now? We can't know from here, since by definition, the virtual is heretofore unknown. The pursuit of the virtual thus involves a risk and a wager (as all good art should).

McKenzie Wark explains, "History is the virtual... made actual... The virtual is not just the potential latent in matter, it is the potential of potential." [39] Galloway and Thacker observe, "The nonbeing of the present moment is by far the hardest thing to imagine... What is it... that hasn't happened, and how could it ever be achieved?" [40]

Playing The Whole Network Surface as An Instrument

"The net as a whole [is] more interesting than any individual art project."– Eddo Stern [41]

I want to return to the practice of artistic surfing (now even more broadly imagined) and explore an additional tactic that might result in an actualization of the virtual. Instead of surfing the entire network and posting the results of your surfing sessions on a single, discrete, compartmentalized (albeit "socially netoworked") platform; I propose the purposeful and systematic dispersion of your wake across multiple nodes of the network via multiple accounts on multiple social networking platforms (multiple private URLs, group photoblogs, Delicious, Flickr, Twitter, Facebook, MySpace, YouTube, Tumblr, etc). The goal is to make the scope of your wake wider than the scope of your personal surfing excursions.

Begin simply, by "playing" Google Image Search as an improvisational instrument. Construct Boolean search queries that auto-bricolage revelatory results. Post these Boolean searches as links throughout the entire network and title them as if they were works of art. Every time someone clicks on your link, they will automatically "perform" a Google search that you have "conducted." The results will vary from week to week depending on Google's image ranking algorithms and other network activity. This tactic produces a very shallow wake, but since these Google Image search "pieces" are so low bandwidth (they are simply text links), they are easily dispersed. You could even write them on pieces of paper and hand them out at the mall. This type of work is similar to Cagean or Fluxus performance instructions. It is as much about language and utterance as it is about "found digital objects."

If you are going to play the entire network as an instrument, you will eventually want to control the search results that people see when they type in targeted words that you choose to hijack. Select a word you want to hijack at Google Image Search and begin propa-

gating your own selected images throughout the network, taxono-
mically associating them with the word you have chosen (via XML
tags, meta-tags, URLs, descriptive body text, file and folder names,
associative linking, etc.) Initially, you will need a small army of col-
laborators to help jump-start this dispersal. Offline performances,
gallery installations, and promotional publicity stunts should also be
enacted in order to generate more press for your meme. Press about
these enacted historical events will be fed back into Google, further
propagating your meme. Once your image/word meme reaches critical viral mass, you won't be able to stop people from dispersing
and modulating your images.

In 1996, eToy's *Digital Hijack* achieved something similar by
hijacking searches for popular words at search engines, gaining high
rankings for those words, and linking people who searched for those
words to their own *Digital Hijack* web site. But this was accompli-
shed with bots and code at a deep level. Accomplish your hijack
with the help of human participation. By the time you hijack the
words you want, it won't be a deep level software "hack;" it will be
a surface level, natural language "hack." Your chosen image results
will appear not because of your coding skills, but because of your
social networking (aka "web 2.0 marketing") skills. Google will
merely be accurately reflecting the popularity of the image/word
meme you have chosen to disperse. The goal is ultimately to "hack"
human language, history, and thought in order to force Google Images to auto-bricolage on your behalf. Your "work" will be perpetually performed every time someone does an image search for the
key word you have hijacked. Rather than artistically surf through a
terrain seeded by corporations, you will be seeding your own emergent terrain through which others will artistically surf. These two

practices (artistic surfing and massively distributed wake seeding) are not mutually exclusive.

Parables For The Hypertrophic

"Saying that politics is an act of 'resistance' was never true, except for the most literal interpretation of conservatism. We must search-and-replace all occurrences of 'resistance' with 'impulsion' or perhaps 'thrust.' Thus the concept of resistance in politics should be superseded by the concept of hypertrophy." - Alex Galloway and Eugene Thacker [42]

Hypertrophy is the unhealthy enlarging of an organ beyond its normal functional capacity. It is a form of modulation and rupture that may cause new uses to emerge. Paul Virilio famously compared the internet to the Titanic: "It is an instrument which performs extraordinarily well but which contains its own catastrophe." [43] I posit that this catastrophe is contained not only at a deep technological level of computer code and hardware, but also at a surface level of uttered language, memes, and cheesy lo-res animations.

It seems unfortunate and unnecessary to segregate the promising moves and tactics of surface level play involved in contemporary artistic surfing practices from the deep level ethical aspirations of earlier net.art practices. And it is indeed a waste to apply de Certeau's critical insights only to art work that identifies itself as "tactical media." Artistic surfing was tailor-made for de Certeauian critical analysis. This paper is a step toward fruitfully applying *The Practice of Everyday Life* to the practice of artistic surfing.

///

This essay was originally presented at *NET.ART (SECOND EPOCH): The Evolution of Artistic Creation in the Net-system. 3rd Inclusiva-net Meeting* (Buenos Aires). Available online in English <http://lab404.com/articles/commodify_your_consumption.pdf> and Spanish <http://medialab-prado.es/mmedia/2016>.

[1] Some active surf clubs as of February 2009: <www.spiritsurfers.net>, <www.loshadka.org/wp/>, <http://doublehappiness.ilikenicethings.com>, <www.supercentral.org>.
[2] David Garcia and Geert Lovink popularized the term "tactical media" in their 1997 article "The ABC of Tactical Media" [http://subsol.c3.hu/subsol_2/contributors2/garcia-lovinktext.html], in which they "poach" their understanding of "tactics" from de Certeau.
[3] Michel de Certeau, *The Practice of Everyday Life* (Berkeley: University of California Press, 1984), 66.
[4] Ibid., 38.
[5] Nicolas Bourriaud, *Postproduction: Culture As Screenplay : How Art Reprograms the World* (New York: Lukas & Sternberg, 2000), 4.
[6] Nato Thompson, "Contributions to a Resistant Visual Culture Glossary," *The Journal of Aesthetics and Protest 1*, no. 3 (2004). URL: <http://journalofaestheticsandprotest.org/3/thompson.htm>.
[7] See Anne-Marie Schleiner, "Fluidities and Oppositions among Curators, Filter Feeders, and Future Artists," *Intelligent Agent 3*, no. 1 (Winter/Spring 2003). URL: <www.intelligentagent.com/archive/Vol3_No1_curation_schleiner.html>.
[8] de Certeau, *Everyday Life*, 34.
[9] A cynical extreme of this position was expressed by Julian Stallabrass in 2003: "It can hardly be expected that people crippled in other walks of life by mass-media trivialisation and the instrumentality of work will be able to slough off such ingrained influences and so realise rational discourse online." (*Internet Art: The Online Clash of Culture and Commerce* (London: Tate Pub., 2003), 67.) I'm not sure that "rational online discourse" is necessarily the ideal goal, but his point is duly noted. Spurse co-founder Iain Kerr says that every time he goes on a derive, he always winds up at a book store. His revolutionary epiphany: he has been conditioned to buy books.
[10] "[Interaction] corresponds to a networked model of control... Many today say that new media technologies are ushering in a new era of enhanced freedom and that technologies of control are waning. We say, on the contrary, that double the communication leads to double the control." (Alexander R. Galloway and Eugene

Thacker, *The Exploit: A Theory of Networks* (Minneapolis: University of Minnesota Press, 2007), 124). Put more acidly, "Since democracy means having more consumer choices, and information technology will vastly increase the power of our channel changers, hey, presto! More democracy!" (Thomas Frank, "The New Gilded Age," *Commodify Your Dissent: Salvos from The Baffler* (New York: Norton, 1997), 28).

[11] "There is really no need in this day and age to create imagery anymore because you can find anything online." (Petra Cortright quoting Oliver Laric. URL of mp3: <http://rhizome.org/events/net_aesthetics/>).

[12] Gilles Deleuze, "Postscript on the Societies of Control," *OCTOBER 59*, (Winter 1992), 3-7. URL: <www.n5m.org/n5m2/media/texts/deleuze.htm>.

[13] There are plenty of early net artists who have always worked at a surface level. Heath Bunting's "Own, Be Owned, or Remain Invisible" <www.irational.org/heath/_readme.html> is a classic example of early surface net art.

[14] Although "web 2.0" tools facilitate current artistic surfing practices, I resist the label "net art 2.0" because it suggests a kind of planned obsolescence, as if it were time for a "refreshing new trend" in net art. This is a convenient way to market new artists to old galleries, but not very historically accurate. If contemporary net art must be saddled with an "x.0" moniker, we should at least be up to 3.0 by now.

[15] Cf. <http://potatoland.org/shredder/>.

[16] Cf. <http://oliverlaric.com/5050.htm>.

[17] de Certeau, *Everyday Life*, 31.

[18] I am admittedly hijacking and mangling Kevin Bewersdorf's strict definition of "wake." According Bewersdorf, a mere link list probably doesn't qualify as a wake, and a found animated gif posted on a group photoblog will more likely be a combination of "boon" and "frame." See "Spirit Surfing," 2008, in Kevin Bewersdorf, *Spirit Surfing*, Link Editions, Brescia 2012, 21 - 26.

[19] See Curt Cloninger's 2002 "traffic_report" project <www.lab404.com/data> which displays the browser histories and referrer logs of participating artists, designers, and writers within a twenty-four hour period.

[20] This observation is a slight modulation of de Certeau's modulation of Kant's analogy of the tightrope walker. See de Certeau, *Everyday Life*, 73, 79.

[21] Ibid., 170.

[22] Vannevar Bush, "As We May Think," *The Atlantic*, (July 1945). URL: <www.theatlantic.com/doc/194507/bush>.

[23] See <www.shiftspace.org>.

[24] See Bewersdorf, "Spirit Surfing", cit.

[25] Quoted by Gary Groth in "A Dream of Perfect Reception: The Movies of Quen-

tin Tarantino," *Commodify Your Dissent*, 183.
[26] In de Certeau's original context, "these practices" are "tales, stories, poems, and treatises." de Certeau, *Everyday Life*, 80.
[27] Ibid., 37-8.
[28]Joshua Decter, "Haim Steinbach (interview, pt. 1)", *Journal of Contemporary Art* 5, no. 2 (1992), 115. Quoted in Peter Schwenger, *The Tears of Things: Melancholy and Physical Objects* (Minneapolis: University of Minnesota Press, 2006), 135.
[29] Quoted in Bruce Hainey, " Haim Steinbach: Sonnabend Gallery, New York," *Artforum 46*, no. 4 (December 2007), 339.
[30] Ibid.
[31] de Certeau, *Everyday Life*, 88.
[32] Deleuze, *Societies of Control*.
[33] Jeffrey T. Nealon, *Foucault Beyond Foucault: Power and Its Intensifications Since 1984* (Stanford, Calif: Stanford University Press, 2008), 110.
[34] Ibid., 98.
[35] Alexander R. Galloway and Eugene Thacker, *The Exploit: A Theory of Networks* (Minneapolis: University of Minnesota Press, 2007), 80.
[36] At least as Jeffrey Nealon interprets Foucault. See Nealon, *Foucault Beyond Foucault*, 105.
[37] Ibid.
[38] Geert Lovink, "Isubmit, Youprofile, WeRank: Deconstructing the Web 2.0 Hype," *New Art Dynamics in Web 2 Mode: First Inclusiva-net Meeting* (Madrid, July 2007), 29. URL: <http://medialab-prado.es/article/documentacion_-_1_encuentro_inclusiva-net>.
[39] McKenzie Wark, *A Hacker Manifesto* (Cambridge, MA: Harvard University Press, 2004), [009, 014].
[40] Galloway, *Exploit*, 133-4.
[41] Paraphrased by Steve Dietz, "Why Have Their Been No Great Net Artists," 1999. URL: <www.afsnitp.dk/onoff/Texts/dietzwhyhavether.html>.
[42] Galloway, *Exploit*, 98.
[43] Paul Virilio, "Infowar," *Ars Electronica*, ed. Timothy Druckery (Cambridge: MIT Press, 1999), 334.

2008
Disontology (God Is No-Thing)

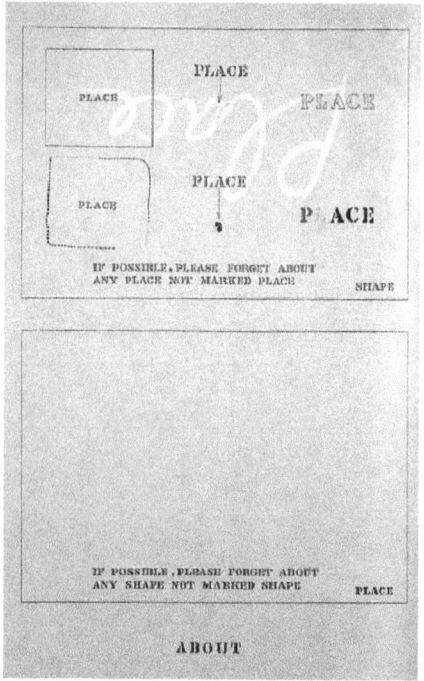

Arakawa + Gins, from the series *Mechanism of Meaning* (15.3), 1963-97, installation view. Published in *Reversible Destiny: Arakawa/gins*. New York: Guggenheim – Museum Publications, 1997.

"Whoever perceives something in God and attaches thereby some name to him, that is not God. God is above names and above nature." *(Eckhart 1981, 204)*

"He is nothing. He is no thing." (Pseudo-Dionysius 1987, 103)

The job of language is inherently reductive. For example, although each pinecone in the world is unique and different, a language that had a different word for every single pinecone would be useless.

Language abstracts the complexities of the world into manageable words. It creates ontological categories, delimiting what it considers to be the important differences, and ignoring what it considers to be the inconsequential differences. Thus English distinguishes between 'pineapple' and 'pinecone,' but not between 'pinecone a' and 'pinecone b.'

The challenge is to keep from reifying words – to avoid thinking of words as the phenomena they abstract. [1] In the famous phrase of philosopher Alfred Korzybski, "A map is not the territory" (Korzybski 1996, 750). [2] Although language is not the exact phenomena it describes, neither is it merely metaphysical. It doesn't simply sit outside of the world and describe it. Instead, language is an active force within the world. It exerts its own agency on humans and historical events. "Apophatic" writers (authors from the historical tradition of Negative Theology) use the agency of language in the world to undermine (and thus balance/leaven) language's more metaphysical, ontological tendencies.

Indo-European languages inherently reduce phenomena in the world to subjects & predicates, action verbs & linking verbs. A subject can act on a predicate ("Dogs chase cats."), or a subject can be a predicate ("Dogs are pets.") The biases of these languages become particularly acute when we use them to describe God, since God is irreducible and un-abstractable. Even when I use language to say "God is irreducible," I am reducing God to a subject described by a predicate adjective. If I say "Language cannot fully describe God," I am reducing God to a predicate acted upon by the subject 'language.' In order to keep from overly reducing God (which is a form of idolatry), each sentence I say about God must be qualified by a subsequent sentence, and that sentence must be qualified by a

subsequent sentence, ad infinitum. Michael Sells calls this apophatic project of using language to un-delimit God "disontology" (Sells
1994, 7). In order to keep words from always having the last word
(and thus delimiting God), we must continually use words to unsay
themselves. This strategy of disontology is a performative one, perpetually deferring any single, final, all-encompassing definition.

Such a telescoping chain of unsaying is more than simply a single
negative assertion. For example, Magritte's famous painterly assertion, "Ceci n'est pas une pipe" (This is not a pipe) is more interested
in exposing "the treachery of images" than in undermining the treachery of words. Had Magritte wished to enact the kind of apophatic
language I'm describing, he might have painted another painting of
the first painting and labeled it "This is not not a pipe," etc.

Prose is a difficult medium in which to enact disontology, because prose is so used to being denotatively meaningful. Deleuze
explains Samuel Beckett's turn away from words and toward music, space, and image: "The reason [Beckett] became increasingly
intolerant of [words]: the exceptional difficulty of 'boring holes in
the surface of language so that 'what lurks behind it' might at last
appear... [Words] are so burdened with calculations and significa-
tions, with intentions and personal memories, with old habits that
cement them together, that one can scarcely bore into the surface
before it closes up again. It imprisons and suffocates us" (Deleuze
1997, 172-3).

Nevertheless, Beckett and apophatic writers like Dionysius and
Meister Eckhart were forever wrestling against the strictures of
prose. This is why their tactics had to be so ingenious and extreme. When these same radical apophatic tactics are applied to the
less denotatively bound media, an even more disruptive form of

apophasis can occur.

One way to avoid the inherent ontological project of language is by using language to perform its 'meaning' rather than merely say its meaning. To perform language is to exert its agency in the world. One overt way to exert the agency of language in the world is to make language explicitly more physical, more embodied. Several supra-prose media strategies achieve this.

Embodied Language via Multimedia Syne-sthesia (eye [h]ear you)

Human/Computer Interface designer Joy Mountford once observed, "When the computer stares back at you, it sees you as one eye and one finger" (Utterback 2004, 218). In other words, we have designed our computer interfaces as if we ourselves are disembodied minds. A corollary might be, "When the book stares back at you, it sees you as one eye." New media art has the capacity to engage much more than our minds, but new media artists must purpose to make work that speaks an embodied language. Particularly promising is new media art that uses language in conjunction with software-controlled animation, audio, video, and physical installation spaces. Such artwork enlists its viewers to experience language in more holistic, less disembodied way. Just as apophatic writing is meant to performatively confound "the mind" of the reader, apophatic new media art confounds the entire body of the viewer.

New media artist Camille Utterback writes, "As we create new interfaces between our bodies and our symbolic systems we are in an unusual position to rethink and re-embody this relationship"

(Utterback 2004, 226). Utterback and Romy Achitiv achieve such a remapping of the relationship between text and body in their piece *Text Rain* (1999). Letters from a pre-selected poem 'rain' down as projections from the top of a screen. Viewers can 'catch' the letters as they fall and hold them (sensors in the room read the viewers' body outlines and feed the coordinates of these outlines into the projection system, causing the letters to 'land' on them). The letters can be gathered as words and phrases, which can then be recombined. Although successful according to the artists' intentions, the weakness of this piece from the perspective of apophatic goals lies in its lack of conceptual coupling between the pre-selected text and the behavior of the system. The text is from a poem about bodies and language (Utterback 2004, 221), but the poem itself is still mimetic – it doesn't embody language. Simply porting such a text, letter by letter, into an embodied multimedia system doesn't magically cause the ontological function of the original text to disappear. Although the interactive system itself is admirably novel, a tighter conceptual coupling between what the text says and what it does is required in order to achieve a more embodied form of language.

Arakawa and Madeline Gins' *The Mechanism of Meaning* (1963-1997) seems far more successful at achieving a phenomenological embodiment of language, and subsequently disrupting it. The piece consists of multiple stations constructed as simple interactive exercises. Each exercise examines a different cognitive aspect of "meaning-making." The exercises are largely text-based, but the text is always situated in a kind of mock-Cartesian painterly space, and its letterforms frequently do more than simply denote. There are always accompanying lines, diagrams, and images, as well as instructions that require bodily (or at least mental) action on the part

of the viewer. Often the exercise stations even extend physically into the gallery space with various apparatuses to be manipulated.

The Mechanism of Meaning succeeds where *Text Rain* fails because the textual 'content' of each of Arakawa and Gins' exercises is tightly and non-arbitrarily coupled with the embodied event they mean to enact. Whereas *Text Rain* might be considered a phenomenological installation with semi-arbitrary text (altering the text doesn't radically alter the phenomenological affect of the piece), *The Mechanism of Meaning* is a phenomenological installation whose text is integral. Indeed, the phenomenological affect of each exercise is created in no small part by the text itself. If we were to extract the text of *Text Rain* from the installation and set it in Helvetica typeface as poetry in a book, its meaning would shift due to the change in context, but it would still maintain the integrity of an English language poem. Whereas, if we were to extract the texts of *The Mechanism of Meaning* from their spatial con-texts and set them in Helvetica typeface as poetry in a book, they would read as alternately facile and meaningless. Likewise, if we were to inject another text into the *Text Rain* installation, the overall impact of the system would remain largely unaltered. Whereas, if we were to inject other texts into *The Mechanism of Meaning*, the impact of the installation would be lost. Although *The Mechanism of Meaning* employs no 'new media' (or even video for that matter), its purposeful and ingenious diagrammatic mechanisms achieve a phenomenological impact that most new media artists only hope to achieve.

Lawrence Weiner is another artist whose language installations don't rely on 'multimedia' or 'interactive media,' but who nevertheless powerfully embodies language by treating it sculpturally. Weiner once wrote,

"Art is not a metaphor upon the relationship of human beings to objects & objects to objects in relation to human beings but a representation of an empirical existing fact. It does not tell the potential & capabilities of an object (material) but presents a reality concerning that relationship." (Bee 2000, 201-202).

It may seem curious that the term 'language' doesn't appear in Weiner's definition of art; but to Weiner, the inclusion of 'language' would be redundant since language itself is simply one more form of sculptural material. Words are the very 'objects' of which he speaks. As such, words are not mere 'metaphors' that 'tell;' they are 'materials' that '[re]present' real relationships in the real world. In his work, Weiner doesn't so much introduce agency to language (language already has agency). Instead, he foregrounds language's agency by giving it a new kind of embodied, sculptural physicality in the world. In so doing, he activates and catalyzes its performative relationship to other objects and to humans. [3]

   Richard Serra and Nancy Holt's *Boomerang* video (1974) [4] is another example of embodied language, this time using tape-delayed audio feedback and spoken words. The speaker in the piece (Nancy Holt) is equipped with headphones and asked to speak into a microphone. Her voice is played back to her through the headphones after about a half-second delay. Watching the video, we see her speaking and listening, and we hear both her original spoken voice and the delayed voice. She narrates her perception of the experience, and as she does the language which she uses to describe the experience perpetuates the experience she is describing. At one point she says, "The words become like things. I'm throwing things out into the world and they are boomeranging back... My mind goes out into the world and then comes back to me." It is telling that Holt associates language not with her voice or her body, but with her disembodied mind. When presented with this disjunctive phenomenological experience of overtly embodied language, she not only experiences language as physical, she also experiences her "mind" as having embodied agency, going "out into the world." This simple experiment suggests further audio/visual strategies for enacting embodied language.

Handwriting as Gestural Voice (Let Your Fingers Do The Talking)

Concrete poetry and other forms of "visual" writing (Mallarmé, Appollinaire, Marinetti, Dada, e.e. cummings, Fluxus) are obviously forms of embodied language – moving beyond the merely denotative, abstracted meaning of words and onto concerns about typography and spatial layout between words on the page. Yet, as critic Johanna Drucker polemically argues, "Very little visual poetry is interesting, but all poetry is interesting in its visuality" (Drucker 2005). Her point is that the 'language' of text has always been affected by its own means of physical production, whether intentionally or accidentally. Currently, with digitally animated typography expressively spinning, morphing, and oozing its way through the title sequences of every new Hollywood movie, after the digital typographic revolution of *Émigré Magazine* and David Carson's shattered *Raygun Magazine* layouts, now that the formal techniques of visual poetry have become production staples of popular media culture, there is no longer anything formally radical about the inten-

tional spacing of words on a page and the intentional use of typography to set words on a page. [5]

Drucker further argues that there is no such thing as a historically generic visual style. Although conceptual artists tried to avoid expressive style altogether, this attempt became inescapably associated with a kind of recognizable 'un-style.' "Lawrence Weiner's stenciled letters on the wall, as industrial and un-aesthetic as he can make them, or John Baldessari's otherwise-empty 1967 canvas bearing the words 'True Beauty' in block letters are striking instances of self-conscious use of graphical codes. A rough-and-unfussy industrialism, uninflected by the artist's hand, un-expressive of emotion or personal voice, provide the distinctive character to conceptual visual language." Drucker goes on to explain,

No one ever accused conceptual artists or writers of over-doing their graphic design. The under-stated and un-inflected attempt at neutrality is now as formulaic and recognizable-as-code as any other set of graphical principles. (Drucker 2005)

From the perspective of embodied language, a neutral graphic style is indeed impossible, since even the most standardized printed page of text is always doing more than it is simply saying. If there is no neutral visual style, then what should a purposefully "embodied" typeface look like? Ideally, a typeface should focus on the physicality of the words in order to apophatically foreground their performativity rather than their ontological function. Human handwriting seems a natural solution. As psychiatrist Hans Prinzhorn observed in his analysis of art by mental patients,

Even the simplest scribble... is, as a manifestation of expressive gestu-res, the bearer of psychic components, and the whole sphere of psychic life lies as if in perspective behind the most insignificant form element. (Rhodes 2000, 63)

Handwriting infuses the physical movement of the artist's hand into the denotative 'meaning' of the word itself. It takes a willful, performative, historical, time-based event – an event during which the writer is thinking the meaning of the word that her hand is inscri-bing – and couples it with the 'word itself.' In this sense, the hand-written word is inscribed with a psychic trace of the internally ima-gined word. Handwriting blurs the line between movement, writing, text, word, syntax, semantics, and semiotics – all the sub-categories into which 'language' might be subdivided.

Several software artists have experimented with hand-drawn line as a form of user input. Golan Levin's *Scribble* performances and his interactive *Yellowtail* software take an initial line gesture drawn by the artist or a user (via mouse or digital pen pad), analyze the nature of the line based on its curves and the speed with which it is drawn, and immediately animate the line in a manner driven by the analysis. If you draw a slow, wiggly, sideways line, your line begins slowly wriggling across the screen. If you draw short, fast, straight, vertical lines, they speed down the screen like rain. Levin's *Alphabet Synthesis Machine* takes similar input – a squiggly written gesture – and interpolates it into an entire "alien" alphabet for the user to download as a digital font.

These pieces fall somewhere between line and letterform, but neither piece is dealing with 'language' in the apophatic sense. Nei-ther piece begins with a denotative, kataphatic statement, so there can be no real apophasis (since a concrete 'saying' is required before

any 'unsaying' can occur). Levin's pieces serve as intriguing prototypes in abstraction and writing-based computational animation – potential formal models for more language-specific conceptual art.

Amit Pitaru's *Sonic Wire Sculpture* comes a bit closer to language-specific art in that it maps hand-drawn lines to audio tones. The user draws lines that are instantaneously spun around a y-axis in virtual 3D space. As each line 'comes around' to the front, it emits a tone. The closer the line is to the top of the screen, the higher the pitch of the tone. A single, gradually undulating line drawn high on the screen sounds like a violin. A series of short dashes drawn low on the screen sounds like bass percussion. Every time the piece revolves around, you can add more lines, gradually composing time-based music via your sense of dimensional space. The piece is inspirationally synesthetic, embodied, and phenomenological; but like Levin's pieces, it lacks any form of ontological source language.

Even closer to proper apophatic art is Diane Gromola's *Biomorphic Typography* – a strange hybrid of generative and typographic systems. Gromola describes the project:

> *The user is hooked up to a biofeedback device that changes the visual character of the font she is writing with in real time. So, for example, the font 'throbs' as the user's heart beats, and grows tendrils and spikes, as the user becomes 'excitable'. (Wardrip-Fruin 2004, 230-31)*

Note: the user is not really 'writing;' she is typing; so the mapping of heart to hand is still mediated via keyboard and typeface. The user is baffled trying to 'read' the typed words to discern their disembodied, ontological meaning while at the same time 'watching' the letterforms of the words expressively move in response to what her body is 'feeling.' Even this strange connection between body and typography was too overtly mapped for Gromola, so she modified the system to give the typography its own autonomous, animated agency in conjunction with the user's biofeedback input. Gromola explains,

If there is no legibility of cause-and-effect, if the interactivity is not legible, I might as well play a videotape. But this intermingling of responsiveness can be a way to sustain awareness and at the same time, to continually provoke different kinds of awareness of autonomic states.

She goes one to wonder, "Do emergent properties need to be perceived as such?" (Wardrip-Fruin 2004, 232). I would answer, "It depends on what one means by 'perceived.'"

In trying to negotiate the continuum between an overtly legible phenomenological experience and an utterly bewildering one, Gromola begins to touch on kataphatic/apophatic concerns. The ideal solution is not to compromise these differences and meet somewhere in the middle, but to somehow allow both extremes to affect the user simultaneously – an experience that is both totally explicable and utterly baffling.

An Object Language (A Language of Objects)

A final argument can be made for a language of objects that includes no words at all. If Weiner is right, if words are objects in the world with their own agency in relation to other objects in the world, if language is a force in the world in relation to other forces in the world, then might non-linguistic objects inversely be treated as words in their own kind of language system? Words relate to and act on other words depending on the ways in which they are arran-

ged, generating 'meaning.' Might objects also be arranged in ways that act on other objects in order to generate 'meaning.'

I don't mean to be so open-ended as to simply claim that there is a 'language' of expressive movement called 'dance' and a 'language' of expressive tone called 'music,' etc. Although these statements are certainly valid in some sense, I am more interested in trying to identify a specific synesthetic syntax of objects in physical proximity to one another. This project is bound to fail from a verifiable, objective, scientific perspective, because objects aren't words in the same way that words are objects. In the song "Smoke Rings" (1986), Laurie Anderson provocatively asks, "Que es mas macho, pineapple or knife?" Our abstracted words for pineapple and knife are categorized as masculine and feminine according to the grammatical rules of Spanish, but the objects themselves don't inherently possess any objective degree of masculinity or femininity. Indeed, do any objects inherently possess any degree of any quality (qualia)? Do humans? What other questions might be raised by attempting to construct even an admittedly subjective language of objects?

Original Chinese ideograms can be thought of as a written language of abstracted objects. But there is nothing terribly apophatic about using a drawing of an inkwell to stand-in for the word 'writing.' More potentially apophatic is creating an embodied language of objects whose syntactic relationship might be 'sensed' but never ontologically delineated. Such an object language shifts the emphasis from the objects themselves to the relationships between the objects to the kind of overall system that might encompass and sustain such relationships as systematically meaningful. But no object-to-English 'translation' need ever be given.

The object ensembles of Fred Wilson and Mark Dion approach

what I'm calling a language of objects, but Wislon's ensembles of museological artifacts tend to be too didactic and metaphorical to meet my criteria for a language of objects (too kataphatic without an apophatic counterpart); while Dion's meticulously arranged ensembles of freshly excavated artifacts tend to be too abstract and painterly to meet my criteria (too apophatic without a kataphatic origin). In all fairness, neither artist is trying to construct an apophatic language of objects. They are pursuing entirely different conceptual goals.

Haim Steinbach's object ensembles come closer to the embodied object language I hope to trace. Indeed, Steinbach claims that objects "have functions for us that are not unlike language" (Decter 1992, 115). His objects are not so much stand-in signifiers for abstract signifieds (colonialism, consumption, New England history, etc.). Instead, because of the strangely purposeful/ purposefully strange way he selects, arranges, displays, and labels them, his objects begin to resonate with each other (to 'speak to' each other) in a way that implies a disontological syntax of embodied sympathies. This syntax has something to do with the physical characteristics of the objects (color, surface material, weight, reflectivity) and something to do with their cultural history (what they are actually used for, what era they connote), but it is not simply a composite of these two components. In some sense, their syntax happens in addition to them. This implicit disontological syntax is also governed by the way the objects are positionally in the world in relation to each other. Steinbach's rigorously constructed shelves and their precise placement on the wall are as much a part of his work as the objects themselves. Fellow sculptor Lisa Lapinski argues, "The shelf works are frac-

tions: the things in the world divided by the minimalist object"
(Hainey 2007, 339).

   All objects are probably related to each other in a similar way, but
we humans aren't used to perceiving these irreducible relationships
(and the objects themselves feel no obligation to disclose them to
our ontological 'minds'). The genius of Steinbach's installations is
that they begin to hint at this mysterious embodied syntax that might
exist amongst all objects. Whether and in what form this syntax of
objects actually exists is ultimately unverifiable, but the mere suggestion of its existence is disontologically thrilling. [6]

Conclusion

   Although God is not a thing to be ontologically categorized,
the ontological language that would describe him is itself a kind
of thing/object/embodied force in the world. The goal of apophatic
art is not to eradicate the denominating, kataphatic function of language. Instead, by foregrounding language's performative function,
apophatic art seeks to have it apophatically unsay itself. Silence
alone will not accomplish this, nor will absurd babbling. Language
must do while it is saying in a way that unsays what it is doing, so
that we may be confounded by what it is (un)doing and (un)saying.

///

This revised chapter was originally presented as part of an MFA thesis (*Apopha-tic Art: Enacting Exhausted Language / Exhausting Enacted Language*, Maine College of Art, Portland, Maine). The dissertation is available online at <http://lab404.com/articles/apophatic_art.pdf>.

[1] The conundrum of a language's inability to fully describe the world is ex-pressed as early as 600 B.C. in the opening lines of Tao Te King: "Nature can never be completely described, for such a description of Nature would have to duplicate Nature. / No Name can fully express what it represents" (Laozi, trans. Bahm). Or in another translation, "The reason which can be reasoned is not the Eternal Reason. / The name which can be named is not the Eternal Name" (Laozi, trans. Chalmers).

[2] Cf: Jorge Louis Borges' paragraph-length short story, "On Exactitude in Science", which describes a 1:1 scale map made by some overzealous carto-graphers (Borges 1999, 320). In *Sylvie and Bruno Concluded*, Lewis Carroll also mentions a fictitious 1:1 scale map: "It has never been spread out, yet," said Mein Herr: "the farmers objected: they said it would cover the whole country, and shut out the sunlight! So we now use the country itself, as its own map, and I assure you it does nearly as well" (Carroll 2006, 138).

[3] Although Weiner is probably the most famous 'sculptor' of language, he is by no means the only one. For example, a number of artists working specifically with Emily Dickinson's poetry have embodied her language sculpturally, Roni Horn and Lesley Dill in particular (Danley 1997).

[4] Available from <www.ubu.com/film/serra.html>.

[5] Even as early as 1961, instruction-based Fluxus artists were intentionally incorporating typography and layout into their overall conceptual approach. Liz Kotz notes that George Brecht's printed event score cards resemble "the space of modern graphic design in [their] complete interpenetration of visual and textual materials – a space that programmatically invades poetry since Mallar-mé" (Kotz 2007, 95).

[6] Art critic Bruce Hainey succinctly and poetically summarizes Steinbach's work: "Wittgenstein begins Philosophical Investigations by quoting Augustine's *Confessions* on the naming of objects. Steinbach pulls his quotations directly from the world; his confessions deranged in glorious 3-D approach the unna-meable."

Works Cited

Arakawa, Shusaku, and Madeline Gins. 1988. *The Mechanism of Meaning*. New York: Abbeville Press.

Bee, Susan, and Mira Schor. 2000. *M/E/A/N/I/N/G An Anthology of Artists' Writings, Theory, and Criticism*. Durham, North Carolina: Duke University Press.

Benson, Bruce Ellis. 2002. *Graven Ideologies: Nietzsche, Derrida & Marion on Modern Idolatry*. Downers Grove, Ill.: InterVarsity Press.

Carroll, Lewis. 2006. *Sylvie and Bruno Concluded*. Paddington, Australia: ReadHowYouWant.com. Available from <www.hoboes.com/html/FireBlade/Carroll/Sylvie/Concluded/>.

Decter, Joshua. 1992. "Haim Steinbach (interview, pt. 1)". *Journal of Contemporary Art 5*, no. 2: 114-22. Quoted in Schwenger, Peter. *The Tears of Things: Melancholy and Physical Objects*, 135. Minneapolis: University of Minnesota Press, 2006.

Deleuze, Gilles. 1997. *The Exhausted. In Essays Critical and Clinical*, 152-174. Minneapolis: University of Minnesota Press.

Drucker, Johanna. 2005. "Un-Visual and Conceptual". *Open Letter: A Canadian Journal of Writing and Theory 12*, no. 7. Edited by Barbara Cole & Lori Emerso. Available from <www.ubu.com/papers/kg_ol_drucker.html>.

Eckhart, Edmund Colledge, and Bernard McGinn. 1981. *Meister Eckhart, the Essential Sermons, Commentaries, Treatises, and Defense*. The Classics of Western Spirituality. New York: Paulist Press.

Hainley, Bruce. 2007. "Haim Steinbach: Sonnabend Gallery, New York". *Artforum 46*, no. 4 (December): 339.

Korzybski, Alfred. 1996. "Science and Sanity: An Introduction to Non-Aristotelian Systems and General Semantics". CD-ROM 1st ed. Englewood, New Jersey: *The International Non-Aristotelian Library Publishing Company*. Available from <http://esgs.free.fr/uk/art/sands.htm>.

Kotz, Liz. 2007. *Words To Be Looked At: Language in 1960s Art*. Cambridge, Mass.: The MIT Press.

Pseudo-Dionysius. 1987. *The Complete Works*. Translated by Jean Leclercq. Mahwah, NJ: Paulist Press.

Rhodes, Colin. 2000. *Outsider Art: Spontaneous Alternatives*. London: Thames & Hudson.

Sells, Michael A. 1994. *The Mystical Languages of Unsaying*. Chicago: The University of Chicago Press.

Utterback, Camille. 2004. "Unusual Positions – Embodied Interaction with Symbolic Spaces". In *First Person: New Media as Story, Performance, and Game*. Edited by Noah Wardrip-Fruin and Pat Harrigan, 218-226. Cambridge, Mass.: The MIT Press.

Wilson, Robert Anton. 2001. "Robert Anton Wilson Explains Everything (or Old Bob Exposes His Ignorance)." Interview on CD. Louisville, Colorado: Sounds True.

2007
Designing
Context

Stefan Sagmeister's mobile columns for Viennese fashion week, 1990, installation views. Published in *Sagmeister: Made You Look*. New York: Booth-Clibborn Editions, 2001.

Up until the late 1800s, a painter could concern himself solely with what occurred within the borders of his canvas. In the biannual Paris Salon art exhibits, paintings were hung floor to ceiling and side by side, piled upon one another. Nobody considered the implications of hanging a painting of a virile bull directly above a painting of a reclining woman, and the artist certainly was not responsible for the overall context in which his work appeared publicly.

It's not that artists in the 1800s were technically unable to control the contexts in which their art appeared, it's just that there was, as yet, no historical precedent for doing so. However, when Marcel Duchamp entered a signed urinal into an art exhibit in 1917, everything changed. From then on, artists have been forced to consider the context in which their work is presented.

Likewise, there may have once been a time when a designer could be concerned only with what occurred within the borders of her cleverly composed layout. However, with the advent of interaction design and ubiquitous computing, that time is passing rapidly. Successful designers must now take into account the contexts in which their designs occur, and control those contexts as much as possible. In other words, contemporary designers must learn to design their own contexts.

In order to control the context in which your design appears you may need to reach beyond the realm of design into fields such as cognitive psychology, marketing and branding, sociology, urban planning, political strategy, environmentally conscious industrial production, curatorial art practices, as well as a host of other "non-design" disciplines. What does designing one's context actually look like? Here are a few instructive examples.

Stefan Sagmeister's Mobile Columns

Designer Stefan Sagmeister was once hired to make posters advertising a fashion event in the city of Vienna. The posters were to

be placed on famous advertising columns in the middle of city. Sagmeister decided he would dress the columns up in fashion gowns as
part of the promotion, but the media buyers failed to reserve the columns in time. Undaunted, Sagmeister made replicas of the columns
and dressed them up in gowns. He also made his columns mobile.
He then hired students to stand inside the columns and move them
around town. Some students would stand still just long enough to
allow people to start reading the posters, and then, they would suddenly move, freaking the readers out. Other students would chase
people down the street. By dressing these very officious-looking columns in the fabrics of fashion and making them mobile, Sagmeister
brought them to life, quite literally. In so doing, he mirrored the way
in which this fashion event would bring the historic city of Vienna to
life. The project got tons of press and was a great success.

A non-contextual designer thinking "inside the frame" would never have arrived at this solution. She would have simply designed
the 2D posters and submitted them. The details of their implementation would have been someone else's problem. By "designing"
the context in which his "design" existed, Sagmeister transformed a
passive poster advertisement into a performative event.

Hans Haacke's Manet-PROJEKT 74

In 1974, conceptual artist Hans Haacke was invited to participate
in an exhibit at the Wallraf-Richartz Museum in Cologne, Germany.
At the time, the museum owned a painting by Manet which had
been donated by an ex-Nazi. Haacke's contribution to the exhibit
consisted of nothing more than framed documentation of the Manet

painting's provenance, which publicly exposed the donor's largely overlooked Nazi history. Haacke's piece was banned from the exhibit, but fellow conceptual artist Daniel Buren later pasted Haacke's documentation onto one of his own pieces in the same exhibit. Upon discovering this, the museum removed the documentation from Buren's piece, however by that time, the damage had been done.

By thinking beyond the hermetic "frame" of their own work, and outward toward the larger institution of the museum and the national past of Germany, Haacke and Buren were practicing institutional critique – a kind of prototypical contextual design. Their art hijacked, and thus redesigned, the context in which it appeared. Of course, not every magazine advertisement needs to critique the magazine in which it appears, but design should at least be in conscious dialogue with its surroundings.

Service Design

In his excellent book *Designing for Interaction*, Dan Saffer defines a service as "a chain of activities that form a process and have value for the end user." [1] By way of example, the cashier in a grocery checkout line performs a service. A service can be thought of as a system of events. Service design is the art of designing the entire context around this system of events. In the case of the grocery checkout line, a service designer would script the interactions between the cashier and the customer. She would also design the cash register interface, the signage for the checkout aisles, and dictate the physical layout of the aisles themselves.

In order to properly design such services, a service designer must take into account the size and nature of the shopping carts, the dimensions of the parking lot, the number of store employees per shift, the store's hours of operation, the location of the store within the city, the amount and types of products on sale in the store, etc. In other words, a service designer must necessarily concern herself with the totality of the context in which the service occurs, and she must design (or at least negotiate) that context appropriately.

Of course, not all design is service design, but it provides an instructive model for all designers. As contemporary forms of design increasingly move toward facilitating interaction between humans, designers will need to intentionally design the contexts in which these interactions occur.

James Turrell's Twilight Arch

James Turrell makes art out of light. The craft of his art is in contextualizing the way in which people experience light in space. In Turrell's piece *Twilight Arch*, the viewer first enters a dark room. As her eyes gradually adjust to the darkness, she perceives a faint blue square on the far wall. When she approaches this blue square, she realizes it's not a blue painting hanging on a wall, but rather a square hole cut through the wall, opening onto another room bathed in blue light.

Turrell leads the viewer through a series of gradual, phenomenological revelations. He controls the viewer's pace as she moves through the space by intentionally designing the overall context in which the artwork is experienced. In fact, Turrell designed an entrance hallway that transitions the viewer from the light of the gallery to the darkness of the viewing room for this specific purpose. The entrance hallway is not technically a part of the art, but it constitutes the context in which it exists, so Turrell purposefully designed it as well.

Bruce Mau's Massive Change Exhibit

Designer Bruce Mau was invited to curate a traveling exhibition on design. Rather than merely designing an exhibit that reinforced the currently delimited, modernist concept of design (Eames chairs, constructivist posters, elegant teapots), Mau took the opportunity to entirely redesign our contemporary understanding of design itself. He called his exhibit *Massive Change*. Its slogan proclaims: "*Massive Change* is not about the world of design; it's about the design of the world." Mau interviewed leading thinkers in fields ranging from media theory to genetic engineering. His exhibit is less concerned with the physical artifacts of design, and more concerned with the ways in which design alters our world.

In his book *Life Style*, Mau writes,

Life doesn't simply happen to us, we produce it. That's what style is. It's producing life. Rather than accepting that life is something that we passively receive, accept, or endure, I believe that life is something we generate… Style is a decision about how we live. Style is not superficial. It is a philosophical project of the deepest order. [2]

To Mau, then, all design is contextual design (to greater or lesser degrees). To put any design into the world at all is to alter the world that contextualizes it.

The professional (and ethical) question remains – are we purposefully seeking to design the contexts that exist around our designs?
Such contextual designing is an admittedly challenging and complicated task. Ideally, it means being involved in the creative process
throughout – from product prototyping to branding, marketing, development, post-production, and distribution. It means engaging in
cross-disciplinary research and collaborating with experts in other
fields. Above all, contextual design means thinking beyond the borders of our gridded templates and out into the messy, daunting, and
intricate world in which we live.

///

This essay was originally posted to the Notes on Design blog (Sessions College,
Tempe, Arizona, US). Available online at <www.sessions.edu/notes-on-design/
designing-context>.

[1] Dan Saffer, *Designing for Interaction: Creating Smart Applications and Clever Devices*, New Riders Pub, 2006.
[2] Bruce Mau (edited by Kyo Maclear with Bart Testa), *Life Style*, Phaidon, London 2005.

2006
2,305 Words On "Sweet Child O' Mine"

Surely the second coming is at hand. Screenshot of ABC News segment, *'Sweet Child O' Mine': Voice of a Generation?*, 2 November 2006.

This article is about the song "Sweet Child O' Mine" by Guns N' Roses. It's also about nihilism, fury, lost innocence and living at the spear tip of a history that's fraying and dissipating into irresolvability with each passing moment. "The darkness drops again; but now I know / That twenty centuries of stony sleep / Were vexed to nightmare by a rocking cradle" (W.B. Yeats). "My best unbeaten brother / That isn't all I see / Oh no, I see a darkness" (W. Oldham).

I will write this entire article with "Sweet Child O' Mine" looping loudly in my headphones. If you can get your hands on a copy of

"Sweet Child O' Mine" and some headphones, I invite you to join me. I always thought G N' R were properly ridiculous, and derided them publicly on more than a few occasions. But I'm not laughing now. Back in the day, I searched in vain through obscure late-'80s college-radio playlists for my generation's rallying anthem a la Alice Cooper's "18" or Blue Cheer's cover of Eddie Cochran's "Summertime Blues." Unbeknownst to me, it was playing on MTV in heavy rotation before my glazed-over, unbelieving eyes. Why couldn't I see it? Was it the hair? Or those lame heavy-metal scarves? And why all the freakin' apostrophes (N' Roses, O' Mine)? No matter. All is forgiven now. Time has washed away the ephemeral bubblegum stupidity of lite-metal L.A. culture to reveal the shining testament of late-modern existentialism that glistens before me.

"Sweet Child" narrates and enacts the latter 20th Century's transition from myopically romantic optimism to increasingly troubling disillusion. It begins with the quintessential pop idealization of some dude's girlfriend, and it ends thrashing amidst the sound and fury of encroaching insignificance. It's like taking your date to the malt shop and winding up in a dark, subterranean catacomb. Little Suzy meets Mephistopheles. Like Tom Sawyer and Becky Thatcher lost in that cave with Injun Joe on the loose. "Sweet Child" is really two songs, and therein lies its ingenious tension. The first part is an innocuously beautiful power-rock love paean. Its indelible harmonic guitar riff has earned it a place on many an aerobics mix tape, and justly so. The mere tone of that unaccompanied riff at the beginning of the song ignites my pop-junkie adrenal glands in a deliciously maudlin way. Not even the opening "yea-ea-e-ah" of "I Want It That Way" can compare. Add the meandering, lyrical bass

line that joins the lick after four bars, and I'm already putty in the song's hands. It's embarrassing to publicly admit. I should be ashamed. And yet I'm proud. Proud, I say! Let he who is without sin cast the first stone.

The lyrics tell of an escapist rock 'n' roll love, devoid of any pragmatic details, as a good pop lyric should be. "Her hair reminds me of a warm safe place, where as a child I'd hi-e-ide / And wait for the thunder and the rain to quietly pass me by." Our heroine is not merely elevated on a pedestal. She's not even a fellow traveler on a journey through some ideal landscape. She is actual geography – an ideal landscape in which to hide. Post-colonial feminist critics would deride Axl for his misogynistic cartography and paternalistic pet-naming. After all, woman is not a land to plunder, conquer and colonize; and she's certainly not a child. Fair enough, but what do you expect from the auteur who penned, "I used to love her, but I had to kill her?"

In defense of "Sweet Child," the woman is his shelter, not his stomping ground. She engulfs and encompasses him. It's actually quite touching, in a write-something-special-in-my-yearbook sort of way. I can see our narrator (not Axl, think Richie Cunningham from "Happy Days") with his Sweet Child at Lover's Lane. "Emily, I'm just sitting here staring at your hair, and it's reminding me of a warm, safe place where as a child I'd hide. As a matter of fact, if I stare too long, I'll probably break down and cry." They embrace tenderly, and then go get a milkshake.

Fast forward to the '80s, and "Sweet Child" is wearing ripped jeans and several Cyndi Lauper-ish bracelets on each arm. She waits for our narrator in the back of the trailer park where he picks her up in a green Impala that he bought cheap from his cousin, Randy.

They cruise to Makeout Point. "Shauna, I'm just sitting here staring at your hair, and it's reminding me of a warm, safe place where as a child I'd hide. As a matter of fact, if I stare too long, I'll probably break down and cry." They hump tenderly, and then go lift a six pack of Schaffer.

So far, so good.

All the while, Slash's guitar playing tells a backstory exceedingly more poignant and evocative than the lyric. At first, he's hesitant to even depart from the song's original riff. It's working; it's gleaming; why ruin a good thing? Then, hesitantly, he releases the side of the pool and eases toward the deep end – gradually, cautiously, never so far away from the safety of the riff that he can't swim back and grab it again. Each lick ventures a bit deeper – a few more variations, a few more departures, and then straight back to the riff.

Two verses of this teasing, and then halfway through the second break he launches into a deft lick of chilling intention that startles and exhilarates. Suddenly we realize he's been having us on, he knows exactly where he's going, and we might be in for a bit of a ride. Then, just as unexpectedly as the guitar melody soared, it's back on the ground again. Why all this cat and mouse? Why not just launch out and wail? It's only a verse/chorus rock ballad that's bound to go nowhere. Thus Slash fishes us in and sets us up for the second half of the song, which shatters the '50s/'80s motif and drops us into the nihilism of postmodernism like Galileo dropped the orange.

The second half begins with a baroque minor-key guitar break that melodically resembles little we've heard thus far. Abrupt, eerie, and odd. No more putzing around. Definitely intentional and interesting, but not exactly impassioned. Perhaps he's saving even more

for later. But what later? If this is the bridge, how will he ever return us to the original song? Of course, he never does. The bridge has been burned. Actually, it's not a bridge at all; it's an extro: birthed by the first half of the song only to be disowned, less like a beloved son and more like a bastard offspring – wasted and exiled. How could it even hope to return? You can't unbake a cake. You can't undo the confluence of historical streams. And you can't return to the unfulfilled promise of modernism. We are left stranded in a Fatherless void that the heroic materialism of late capitalism is impotent to fill.

The falcon cannot hear the falconer;
Things fall apart; the centre cannot hold;
Mere anarchy is loosed upon the world,
The blood-dimmed tide is loosed, and everywhere
The ceremony of innocence is drowned;
The best lack all conviction, while the worst
Are full of passionate intensity. —W. B. Yeats

The unsettling culmination of Slash's solo wails this hollowness home. The gloves are off, the sleeper awakes, and wanky pop-metal arpeggiating gives way to genre-defying, wah-wah-drenched fury. No longer anchored by the strictures and certainty of a structure that proved rotten and false, Slash's melody lashes out at the darkness, comes up empty, and lashes out again. Over and over, like the neglected cry of some abandoned creature, like the grasping arms of a drowning man.

Seemingly exhausted, the guitar drops and our narrator's voice resurfaces – deep, growling, and utterly changed. No more eyes of the bluest skies, no more smiles of childhood memories. Just a simple question, over and over. He's asking his beloved, and he's asking

us. He wants to believe. He wants to keep on making pop records where boy meets girl and the DJ spins the tale. He wants to write intelligent articles for optimistic rock 'n' roll magazines that negotiate the fine line between celebrating music and commodifying it. But first he must ask a simple question, over and over: "Where do we go now?"

The question repeats and builds, until it breaks loose into a falsetto wail, re-joined by the guitar, which amplifies and annotates it. The whole imprecatory riot crescendos in an epic complaint that demands an answer it knows it will never get. Twenty years later, here, at the edge of the future, we still don't have an answer. Some of us have even given up asking the question. "Here we are now / Entertain us."

My cynical Marxist friend says, "Rock 'n' roll will never die as long as you have a product to buy." And yet I find myself up all night looping "Sweet Child O' Mine," struggling to explain its brilliance in a way that invites all creatures great and small to rally around its shining profundity – a weathered, defiant, still-flying banner of existential refusal. Am I a loon for finding sublimity in something so sappy?

Yes and no. *Spinal Tap*'s Nigel Tufnel brilliantly observes, "There's a fine line between stupid and clever." Sublimity and sappiness exist side by side. Good sublime art risks sappiness, but avoids it. Great sublime art is simultaneously sappy and sublime; its sappiness makes it all the more sublime. I know I should laugh at such art, and the fact that I'm crying makes me cry all the more. The original BBC episodes of *The Office* are saturated with this kind of sappy sublimity. David Brent's reading of John Betjeman's "Slough" brings me to tears every time.

Come, friendly bombs and fall on Slough
To get it ready for the plough.
The cabbages are coming now;
The earth exhales.

Likewise, the best pop music is always somewhat stupid. Lowell George of *Little Feat* described pop music as "smart/dumb"– smart and dumb at the same time. Smile lyricist Van Dyke Parks concurs: "Just as the best comic books can turn cliché into high art, so can the best pop music. Brian [Wilson] does that. He can take common or hackneyed material and raise it from a low place to the highest, and he can do it with an economy of imagery that speaks to the casual observer – bam!"

The "bam" of "Sweet Child O' Mine" is in Slash's guitar playing. It's one thing to write an essay bemoaning the de-centering of contemporary humankind in a postmodern society. It's another thing entirely to play a wailing guitar solo that viscerally embodies that de-centering. Psychoanalyst Jacques Lacan said we are born into a world of pure being, which language cannot fully express, so we are always longing for a Real we can't describe. Slash's solo doesn't describe this Real, but it compassionately describes the longing we feel at having been severed from it. Without the words to properly express our estrangement, what can we do but wail? Paul of Tarsus wrote, "We do not know what we ought to pray for, but the Spirit himself intercedes for us with groans that words cannot express." The guitar solo at the end of "Sweet Child" intercedes with groans that words cannot express.

But whom does it beseech? To whom does it pray? Slash's solo is not the heroic voice of the Nietzschean atheist, defiant to the end in

his renunciation of the Christian worldview. Nor is it the would-be voice of Dylan Thomas's dying father from "Do Not Go Gentle Into That Good Night," raging against the dying of the light. Nor is it the whimpering voice of the defeated warriors and their hounds from Ezra Pound's "The Return."

These were the swift to harry;
These the keen-scented;
These were the souls of blood.
Slow on the leash,
pallid the leash-men!

Instead, Slash's solo is our voice – 2,000 years after a resurrection we never witnessed, facing a future that seems more or less insoluble. We're not deluded into believing we can return to the idealized modernism of the '50s. And still we're not yet willing to throw in the towel and succumb to nihilistic despair. We still hope beyond hope. We groan. We struggle. And we cry out – not defiantly into the void and not to some man-diluted, manufactured god who can't satisfy. We cry out to the God we hope is actually there. Paul Simon sings,

The rage of love turns inward
To prayers of devotion
And these prayers are
The constant road across the wilderness
These prayers are
These prayers are the memory of God
The memory of God

Slash's solo is fueled by the despair and desperation and painful longing of these prayers.

Most pop songs settle for an escapist visit to Lover Land. "Stay lady stay / Stay while the night is still ahead." "We've got tonight / Who needs tomorrow?" Admittedly, such escapism doesn't solve the world's problems, but it's better than one of Mogwai's interminably angsty, post-rock instrumentals.

"Sweet Child O' Mine" is brave enough not to take sides. It doesn't simply pin its hopes for the satisfaction of mankind on idealized romantic love and a big brass bed. Nor does it mow over the daises and burn down the malt shop. It does something more complex and ultimately more redemptive. "Sweet Child" posits an ideal worth fighting for, admits that the ideal is not currently achievable, and dares to ask, "Why the discrepancy?" This question continues to echo unanswered from shitty dashboard radios tuned to shitty classic-rock stations in shitty green Impalas throughout our land.

"Tom's days were days of splendor and exultation to him, but his nights were seasons of horror. Injun Joe infested all his dreams, and always with doom in his eye."

A shape with lion body and the head of a man,
A gaze blank and pitiless as the sun,
Is moving its slow thighs, while all about it
Reel shadows of the indignant desert birds.
The darkness drops again; but now I know
That twenty centuries of stony sleep
were vexed to nightmare by a rocking cradle,
and what rough beast, its hour come round at last,
Slouches towards Bethlehem to be born? —W.B. Yeats

Where do we go now?

///

This essay was originally published in *Paste Magazine*, online and in print (Avondale Estates, Georgia, US). Available online at <www.pastemagazine.com/ articles/2006/11/2305-words-on-sweet-child-o-mine.html>. You can watch Curt Cloninger read an abridged version of this essay on *ABC News*, at <http://abc-news.go.com/Video/playerIndex?id=2624538>.

2005
Eternity in an Instant: The Moving Images of David Crawford

David Crawford, Frames from *Stop Motion Studies*: Series #8, Sequence #2 and #13, 2004. Courtesy of the artist.

New Media" is a woefully malleable term that generally means "newer than film." Computers are usually involved. But of course "new" is a vague and relative adjective not inherently related to film or computers. New media in its truest sense is simply media that communicates in a new way, a way that previous media could not. By this definition, Etienne-Jules Marey's chronophotography was new media, as was film which followed it. By the same measure, David Crawford's *Stop Motion Studies* series is new media in the truest sense, because like Marey, Crawford is exploring the liminal timescape between still photography and film. What makes *Stop Motion Studies* especially "new" is its peculiar addition of randomizing software.

Crawford's microcosmic photographic studies of (mostly) people (mostly) riding on subways might initially seem like looping micro-films. But upon closer inspection, one realizes that the animations never actually loop. Imagine a slide projector tray filled with anywhere between three to eight slides. The projector displays these same slides infinitely, but always in random order. The projector also randomizes the duration each slide is displayed, anywhere from .03 seconds to .3 seconds (give or take a bit). Finally, all the slides in the tray are of the same subject, all photographed within a limited time frame (less than two minutes). This roughly approximates the mechanics of what Crawford has termed "algorithmic montage." The result is a kind of stochastic motion study more akin to chronophotography than film; but with a distinct, non-linear twist.

Chronophotography was intent upon peering into previously invisible sequences of micro-moments in order to unpack the mysteries of bodies in motion through time. In Crawford's own words, "The work of... Marey compels us to open up, inhabit, and reconsider the density and wonder of the natural world by nature of its interpretation and interpolation of time." [1] Marey was not out to replicate the illusion of motion. On the contrary, he sought to demystify its illusion so that he might better contemplate its subtleties in stasis, at leisure. In this sense, chronophotography is at odds with film – a kind of dissection without any attempt at simulation. D.W. Griffith and his ilk found the illusion of simulation so captivating, they refashioned the research tool that film might have become into the spectacularized storytelling medium that narrative Hollywood film has become. Film increased; chronophotography decreased.

Such is the now familiar tale of advances in technology rendering previous technological experiments irrelevant. But experiments have a way of resurfacing in technological cycles, because each new medium comes with its own set of aesthetic limitations. In Crawford's case, he was forced by the limitations (bandwidth) of his new technology (the internet) to minimalistically re-examine the

original themes of chronophotography from a post-film perspective. Bandwidth limitations in 2002 made Hollywood-genre web video an impossibility, so Crawford took a novel approach. He began experimenting with a digital still camera in burst mode. It could take up to 64 frames per minute. Hardly film quality. Furthermore, 64 high resolution images would take a prohibitive time to download. Part of the solution was to select 3-8 quintessential frames from each batch.

A major obstacle still remained: how to animate these few frames in a way that somehow created a semblance of motion over time? Simply displaying the few frames in chronological order at a set rate would result in what would only seem like crippled film. The solution was Macromedia Flash software with its ActionScript programming language. Crawford was able to program the software to randomize his frame order and frame duration. This resulted in a re-animation of the original static images that refuses both Russian Avant-Garde and Narrative Hollywood film conventions. Whereas the goal of a Hollywood epic like *El Cid* is to distill a lifetime of events into a few hours, the goal of Crawford's work is to expand a micro-moment into infinity. If, as Crawford observes, "Marey's chronophotographs flourished in the tiny space between the still and the moving image," [2] then *Stop Motion Studies* re-inhabits that tiny space, animates it non-linearly, and thus explores it indefinitely.

Crawford's method of using software to randomize this animation process is admittedly a form of artifice, but no more so than film projected at 30 frames per second is a form of artifice. And since fiction is a lie that tells the truth, Crawford's fictive "new media" genre of stochastic animation seems in many ways more "truthful" than documentary film or photojournalistic still photography. What

aspects of the real does *Stop Motion Studies* reveal? First, it reveals the compressed nature of modern space that has become all but invisible to us. Second, it reveals alarming and disarming characteristics of time – time as a construction of human consciousness rather than time as a divisible ontological entity. Finally, and most apparently, *Stop Motion Studies* affords a unique glimpse into the people who are its subjects – a window into their souls previously invisible to both film and still photography. Crawford's project is ultimately less about subways and cities and film history and computer software than it is about human souls in space and time.

Space

"A road is a flattened-out wheel, rolled up in the belly of an airplane."
- Marshall McLuhan [3]

The micro-scenes in *Stop Motion Studies* take place largely on subway trains, and this transitory "stage" is the perfect locale for exploring the subjectivity of time. The fast speed of the trains provides a visual foil for the slow speed of the people on the trains. The people may move very little within their few allotted frames, while outside the world races past in a blur. Yet since the frames are displayed randomly, any sense of continual, linear motion is lost. The trains literally appear to be going nowhere fast. Like Zeno's paradoxical arrow, the trains are perpetually in motion, and yet they never arrive. This underscores the empathy we feel for the passengers who are trapped in a kind of modern purgatory – an in-between time/space they perfunctorily inhabit on their way from "somewhere" to "somewhere else."

Crawford's stochastic animations have a way of ephemerizing even the people themselves. In one frame, a woman is a solid figure, and suddenly in the next she's a blur. The overall effect is reminiscent of Ezra Pound's "In a Station of the Metro" – "The apparition of these faces in the crowd; / Petals on a wet, black bough." Back and forth the woman mysteriously transitions. Neither frame is given chronological or hierarchical primacy. Is the woman "really" there or gone? She is perpetually both. In this sense, "Stop Motion Studies" becomes a formal tool for analyzing, unpacking, and coming to terms with the extreme compressions and expansions of "standard" space/time that modern modes of transportation have thrust upon us.

Still photography is impotent to unpack and analyze such fluidities of time. It freezes the instant to such a point that all time is removed (except for the residual symbolic blur). Standard film is likewise impotent to objectively analyze such relative contractions and expansions of time, because film itself (whether "real-time," slow-motion, fast-forward, or time-lapsed) is always subject to a mechanical version of artificially uniform, linear time. As Paul Virilio says,

Cinema is the end in which the dominant philosophies and arts have come to confuse and lose themselves, a sort of primordial mixing of the human soul and the languages of the motor-soul. [4]

Just as a well-trained son wouldn't publicly criticize his father, the motor-driven projector spool is faithful to the "reality" of the motor-driven wheel. It takes a new medium like algorithmic montage to re-present such fluidities of time and space with a more penetrating, dispassionate eye.

Time

"Human existence de Selby has defined as 'a succession of static experiences each infinitely brief', a conception which he is thought to have arrived at from examining some old cinematograph films which belonged probably to his nephew [These are evidently the same films which he mentions... as having 'a strong repetitive element' and as being 'tedious'. Apparently he had examined them patiently picture by picture and imagined that they would be screened in the same way, failing at that time to grasp the principle of the cinematograph.] From this premise he discounts the reality or truth of any progression or serialism in life, denies that time can pass as such in the accepted sense and attributes to hallucinations the commonly experienced sensation of progression as, for instance, in journeying from one place to another or even 'living'... Thus motion is also an illusion. He mentions that almost any photograph is conclusive proof of his teachings." – The narrator from The Third Policeman [5]

De Selby is a fictional character, nevertheless I wonder what he would have made of *Stop Motion Studies*. Would he have discovered in it something more than a mere "succession of static experiences?" *Stop Motion Studies* is unique in that it is simultaneously momentary and eternal. How does one discover infinity in a microsecond? Again we're back to Zeno's paradoxes. According to the professor from Haruki Murakami's *Hard-Boiled Wonderland and the End of the World*, "Expandin' human time doesn't make you immortal; it's subdividin' time that does the trick." [6]

William Blake's "Auguries of Innocence" famously begins:

To see a World in a Grain of Sand
And a Heaven in a Wild Flower,
Hold Infinity in the palm of your hand
And Eternity in an hour.

Finally, William Burroughs, commenting on his tape cut-up experiments with Brion Gysin, observes that "when you cut into the present, the future leaks out." [7] In the case of *Stop Motion Studies* it's not the future per se, but infinity.

I'm reminded of the machine in Ridley Scott's *Blade Runner* that can zoom in on a high-resolution snapshot to almost infinite detail. There is something slightly terrifying about unpacking a static moment that initially seemed flat and relatively fathomable (a photographic snapshot) only to discover an infinite amount of heretofore subliminal information encoded within it. Such unpacking seems an almost alchemical process – making the invisible visible. *Stop Motion Studies* unpacks similar instances of time into animations that become increasingly resonant and profound as they play out. If this kind of infinity and subtlety can be contained within a seemingly insignificant instant, how many more infinities and subtleties are contained in as many instances? Life gradually begins to seem more pregnant and wondrous.

In this sense, the vignettes in *Stop Motion Studies* are like mnemonic atom bombs. Microcosmic temporalities are split, triggering a chain reaction of macrocosmic revelations. Yet even this metaphor begs the question, do discrete particles of time even exist? Is time atomic, or is it something else entirely? If de Selby (and pop physicists like Peter Lynds) are correct, time may be a whole lot less discrete/concrete than we imagine. It may have more to do with the way human consciousness copes with change. If so, art may prove to be a more nimble and adroit explorer of time than science.

People

" I got us on a hiway, I got us in a car
Got us going faster than we've ever gone before
And I know it ain't gonna last
When I see your eyes arrive
they explode like two bugs on glass."
- Mercury Rev [8]

More than anything *Stop Motion Studies* is a series of human character studies – through the lens of a new and refreshingly empathetic medium, but also through the artist's own empathetic eye. Crawford's aesthetic eye as a photographer and editor is as responsible for the success of the work as his novel coding hack. He is always searching for that precious instance, that essential expressive gesture.

In this sense, *Stop Motion Studies* owes a greater debt to Eadweard Muybridge's *Animal Locomotion* than to Marey's *Animal Mechanism*. Although both men purported to be scientists, Marey was the one actually intent on recording the anatomical motion beneath the surface of human emotion. He even dressed his subjects in black suits and highlighted their limbs in order to focus on formal motion rather than surface personality. Marey was uninterested in analyzing the metaphysical realm (as evidenced by his opposition to the "vitalistic" theories of his era). Whereas the enduring legacy of Muybridge's work stems from his highly aestheticized portrayal of human beings involved in daily tasks (albeit half-naked and in front of a quasi-scientific grid).

Crawford's production process for *Stop Motion Studies* may share Marey's rigor, formalism, and single camera perspective, but the

soulish human realm that *Stop Motion Studies* ultimately unearths and foregrounds is pure Muybridge. Marey wanted to know: How can a sequential arrangement of images unlock nature's secrets in relation to motion? *Stop Motion Studies* asks a similar but distinct question: How can a stochastic arrangement of images unlock nature's secrets in relation to human persona?

Ultimately *Stop Motion Studies* reveals not ideals or grand themes, but individuals. This is both its charm and its melancholy. In every city visited (Boston, New York, Paris, Tokyo) we find characters of distinction, verve, and even nobility; yet they are all going nowhere fast. As these micro-instances unravel before us and we begin to glimpse the wonder and beauty contained within each moment, most of the actual subjects are oblivious to the import of "their own" moments. If only they could see themselves through the lens of this new medium, surely their next commute would be a more enthralling experience! Nevertheless, for those of us willing to spend some time "out of time" meditating on these hidden instances, *Stop Motion Studies* exhorts us to be more fully present and alive in our own moments – however ephemeral, compressed, and in-between they may be.

///

This essay was commissioned for the "Sequences" exhibition and published in the book *Sequences: Contemporary Chronophotography and Experimental Digital Art. Imagetime* (London: Wallflower Press). Available online at <http://lab404.com/articles/sms/>.

[1] David Crawford, *Algorithmic Montage* (Göteborg, Sweden: Master's thesis, IT University Of Gothenburg, 2004), 27.
[2] Ibid., 26.
[3] Marshall McLuhan, McLuhanisms <www.marshallmcluhan.com/mcluhanisms/>.
[4] Paul Virilio, *The Aesthetics of Disappearance* (New York: Semiotext(e) Books, 1991), Part IV.
[5] Flann O'Brien, *The Third Policeman* (Chicago: Dalkey Archive, 1967), chap. 4.
[6] Haruki Murakami, *Hard-Boiled Wonderland and the End of the World*, trans. Alfred Birnbaum (Tokyo: Kodansha International, 1991), chap. 27.
[7] William Burroughs, *Origin and Theory of the Tape Cut-Ups from a lecture given at the Jack Kerouac School of Disembodied Poetics at Naropa Institute*, April 20, 1976.
[8] Jonathan Donahue, lyrics from "Goddess on a Hiway," *Deserter's Songs by Mercury Rev* (New York: V2 Records, 1998).

2004

Even Better Than the [Ethe]real Thing: a Response to Alex Galloway's *Protocol*

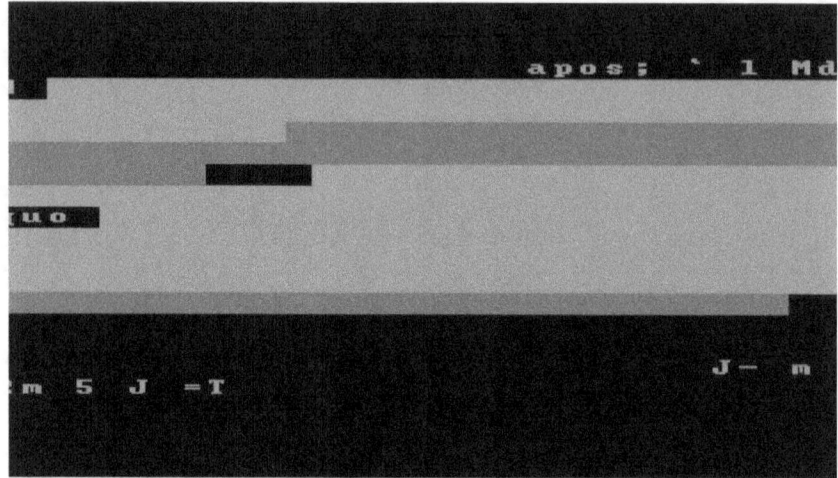

RSG (Radical Software Group), from the *Carnivore* project, 2000. Screenshot of "The Carnivore Personal Edition Zero Client (serial number RSG-CPE0C-1)." Surveillance packets on
a local network are printed to the screen left-to-right, top-to-bottom, in a pseudo random
fashion. Courtesy of the artists.

*All of us were slowly losing that intellectual light that allows you
always to tell the similar from the identical, the metaphorical from
the real. We were losing that mysterious and bright and most beautiful
ability to say that Signor A has grown bestial – without thinking for
a moment that he now has fur and fangs. - Casaubon from Umberto
Eco's Foucault's Pendulum*

Alex Galloway Is a Geek. It's a Good Thing

When reading a text on media theory, my underlying skeptical
question is always, "How much do the nuances which are fore-
grounded and analyzed here practically relate to human experience
and human society?" If they barely do, the book winds up being

one more exercise in scatological academia and/or cyber-utopian fluff-urism. Refreshingly, Alex Galloway's *Protocol* succeeds in avoiding what Geert Lovink calls "vapor theory." This is due in no small part to the fact that Alex Galloway is a geek (or at least a wanna-be geek). Not "geek" in the pejorative sense, but "geek" in the "down with the root workings of technology" sense. For example, Galloway's research led him to read hundreds of RFC (Requests for Comments) documents, the technical documents that establish Internet protocol (among other things). Galloway writes, "Far more than mere technical documentation, however, the RFCs are a discursive treasure trove for the critical theorist." I wonder how many other critical theorists would think so.

Observation, interpretation, and application are the three steps of inductive textual criticism. Not a few technological pundits breeze through the initial observation step, acquiring only a superficial understanding of the tech, and then rush off to boldly interpret and apply. This leads to elaborate, inventive conclusions that are frequently misguided if not altogether wrong. But Galloway has looked long and hard at the network and its protocol, and his interpretations (even though I disagree with some of them) are more intricate and less cliche as a result of his having looked. As such, *Protocol* lays the groundwork for anyone to riff off of Galloway's insightful observations, even if her preconceived biases differ from his.

Furthermore, Galloway's range of sources is so diverse, it feels like an academic compilation tape. His research is intimidatingly broad – from usability expert Jeff Veen to generative software artist Adrian Ward, from open source evangelist Richard Stallman to cult lawyer Lawrence Lessig. Marx, Baudrillard, Barthes, Foucault, and Deleuze make expected appearances. But also appearing are Mar-

xist media theorist Hans Magnus Enzensberger, cyberfeminist Doll Yoko, and phone phreaker Knight Lightning. The list goes on (and on and on).

Furthermore, *Protocol*'s tangential anecdotes about the formation of the internet and the history of hacking and virii read like a scattershot compendium of geek folklore.

Heavy Insights, Well Codified

Galloway's prose, although not exactly McLuhan-esque, is inordinately sound-bytable. Below are just a few "spoilers," nuggets of particularly acute and concise insight.

On the nature of protocol:

"From a formal perspective, protocol is a type of object. It is a very special kind of object. Protocol is a universal description language for objects... Protocol does not produce or causally effect objects, but rather is a structuring agent that appears as the result of a set of object dispositions. Protocol is the reason that the internet works and performs work... It is etiquette for autonomous agents. It is the chivalry of the object."

Note the rare combination of precise description and poetic flair. "The chivalry of the object" is a definite keeper.

On protocol's inherent imperviousness to Modern criticism:

"Only the participants [of protocol] can connect, and therefore, by definition, there can be no resistance to protocol... Opposing protocol is like opposing gravity – there is nothing that says it can't be done, but such a pursuit is surely misguided and in the end hasn't hurt gravity very much."

Along the same lines:

"The internet can survive [nuclear] attacks not because it is stronger than the opposition, but precisely because it is weaker. The Internet has a different diagram than a nuclear attack does; it is in a different shape. And that new shape happens to be immune to the older."

Galloway rightly insists that just as code is more than a mere semantic language (it causes machines to actually do something), the network is more than just a metaphor for connectivity (it actually behaves according to protocol). He instructively traces of the cultural perception of computer viruses – from a form of intellectual exploration to a form of machinic contagion (akin to AIDS) to a form of terrorist weapon. He makes the important distinction between protocol and proprietary market dominance (Windows XP is not a form of protocol because its source code is opaque). And he offers these inspirationally punk rock samples regarding tactical media:

"Everyone interested in an emancipated media should be a manipulator."
"Fear of being swallowed up by the system is a sign of weakness."
"The best tactical response to protocol is not resistance but hypertrophy."

All culminating in this rousing definition:

"The goal is not to destroy technology in some neo-Luddite delusion, but to push it into a state of hypertrophy, further than it is meant to go. Then, in its injured, sore, and unguarded condition, technology may be sculpted anew into something better, something in closer agreement with the real wants and desires of its users. This is the goal of tactical media."

Right on! Where do I sign?

Epistemology Is As Epistemology Does

Having sufficiently praised *Protocol*, I'd like to enter into critical dialogue with it. My first problem with the text is that it oversteps its stated scope. Galloway makes epistemological assertions without offering epistemological defenses. He says in the introduction,

"I draw a critical distinction between [the] body of work [that deals with artificial intelligence], which is concerned largely with epistemology and cognitive science, and the critical media theory that inspires this book. Where the former are concerned with minds and questions epistemological, I am largely concerned with bodies and the material stratum of computer technology."

Unfortunately, "bodies" and "matter" to Galloway take on markedly metaphysical meanings, meanings that delineate a fairly explicit view of reality which he feels no obligation to defend. He asserts a kind of "aesthetic materialism" (his term). In short, he seeks to recast the spiritual and soulish in terms of the "virtual," the "second nature," the cultural/sociopolitical, the "artificial," a "patina," the essence or sheen that derives from matter but is not "other than" matter. (More on this later.)

Protocol eschews epistemological questions as not pertinent to its scope, but by deeming such questions irrelevant, Galloway has already entered into implicit dialogue on "the matter" (pun intended). If I wish to discuss human origins without talking about evolution, I'm a creationist. If I wish to discuss life without talking about soul or spirit, I'm a materialist.

In the book's foreword, Eugene Thacker calls *Protocol* a type of "materialist media studies." He goes on to observe, quite accurately:

"*Protocol* consistently makes a case for a material understanding of technology. 'Material' can be taken in all sense of the term, as an ontological category as well as a political and economic one." Galloway gladly owns up to politics and economics, but his ventures into ontology, although apparent, are less disclosed.

Marx Said It, I Deconstruct It, That Settles It

My next critique of *Protocol* is that it awkwardly uses Marx's *Capital* to justify a contemporary materialist understanding of artificial life.

After 14 pages of foregrounding Marx's vitalistic language, Galloway concludes,

"Capital is an aesthetic object. The confluence of different discourses in Capital, both vitalistic and economic, proves this. The use of vitalistic imagery, no matter how marginalized within the text, quite literally aestheticizes capitalism."

That poetic language can transform a theoretical text into an aesthetic object seems perfectly plausible. That poetic language can "literally aestheticize" capitalism itself is a more vague and suspect assertion.

Even if Marx does attribute a kind of "will" to objects within capitalism, he's not exactly celebrating reification or commodity fetishism. Galloway asserts, "[The] vitalism in Marx heralds the dawning age of protocol, I argue, by transforming life itself into an aesthetic object." Aside from the fact that "life itself" was understood as an aesthetic object in the soulish realm long before Marx, likening commodity fetishism to machinic artificial life seems an awkward stretch. Galloway himself points out that Foucault's theories of control date Marx's, and Deleuze's date Foucault's. Is Marx so canonical that he's worth 14 pages of deconstruction in order to claim him as the historical genesis of one's contemporary assertion?

Dumbing Down Life

Continuing on the "artificial life" critique (and invariably stepping on dozens of cyber-toes), there are two ways to make "computers" seem more than what they are. You can discern life where there is none, or you can redefine "life" until it matches what you discern in computers. Galloway subtly snubs futurist Ray Kurzweil and the *Wired* "gee whiz" crowd for doing the former, and then proceeds to do the latter.

Building on Foucault and Deleuze, Galloway asserts that "life, hitherto considered an effuse, immaterial essence, has become matter, due to its increased imbrication with protocol forces."

He assents to Crary and Winter's definition of "protocological" life as "the forces – aesthetic, technical, political, sexual – with which things combine in order to form novel aggregates of pattern and behavior."

After an explication of Norbert Weiner's ideas on cybernetics, Galloway concludes, "If one views the world in terms of information..., then there is little instrumental difference between man and machine since both are able to affect dynamic systems via feedback loops." Would Weiner himself have agreed to such a sweeping generalization?

So matter is life and life is matter. Not metaphorically, but actually. This is achieved by defining "life" very loosely.

I'm reminded of a passage in *The Language of New Media* where Lev Manovich comes very close to defining "narrative" as any action that constitutes a change of state. Walking from room to room thus becomes a narrative. At which point I would simply choose a different word.

Aesthetic Materialism and the Cyborgs from Mars

Why is Galloway so keen to show that a "second nature" of aesthetic materialism exists in both social and machinic systems? Because such a "second nature" affords the exploration of an aesthetic realm without the abandonment of a materialist world view. Such a "second nature" also admits the possibility of man/machine hybridization. If reality is all just matter, and matter may be abstracted into organized information, artificial life and biological life are "virtually" kissing cousins. Galloway actually defines the information age as "that moment in history when matter itself is understood in terms of information or code. At this historical moment, protocol becomes a controlling force in social life."

At the end of his chapter on "control," Galloway goes on to predict a historical period "after distribution" – a future where computers are replaced by bioinformatics, information is replaced by life, protocol is replaced by physics, and containment is replaced by peace.

A similar "gee whiz" passage occurs earlier in the "control" chapter:

"When Watson and Crick discovered DNA..., they prove not simply that life is an informatic object..., but rather that life is an aesthetic object; it is a double helix, an elegant, hyper-Platonic form that rises like a ladder into the heights of aesthetic purity. Life was no longer a 'pair of ragged claws / Scuttling across the floors of silent seas' (Eliot), it was a code borne from pure mathematics, an object of aesthetic beauty, a double helix! This historical moment – when life is defined no longer as essence, but as code – is the moment when life becomes a medium."

I agree that DNA is fascinating stuff, but to attribute the mystery and wonder of existence to the aesthetic beauty of a DNA strand seems more like cyber-utopian poetry and less like scholarship aloof from ontological concerns.

Elsewhere, Galloway waxes eloquent about biometrics:

"Biometrics [the science of measuring the human body and deriving digital signatures from it] considers living human bodies not in their immaterial essences, or souls, or what have you, but in terms of quantifiable, recordable, enumerable, and encodable characteristics. It considers life as an aesthetic object. It is the natural evolution of Marx's theory of second nature."

The progression from souls to quantifiable biometric information is presented as an aesthetic advancement? If anything, biometrics seems a neo-techno form of alienation.

Another curious assertion: "Computer use could possibly constitute a real immigration of bodies (from the online to the offline)," which seems akin to this cryptic statement by feminist Sadie Plant: "You can't get out of matter, that's the crucial thing. But you can get out of the confining organization of matter which is shaped into things and of course, organisms." I find it difficult to accept such conceptions of the self at face value.

It's The People, People

Protocol radically posits that the Internet is successful not just because it is anarchic, but because this "anarchy" coexists with a rigid form of control. I agree, but I think the rigid form of control is not the DNS (Domain Name System) hierarchy (as Galloway proposes), but the core, old-boy geek community of RFC-writing protocol-shapers (which Galloway critiques as an institutional weakness of protocol). Domain names are a mnemonic convenience, but their use is not a prerequisite for entry to the network. One can still access a server using its IP number, it's just inconvenient. Yet protocols, according to Galloway's definition, are not merely meant to make access more convenient, they are meant to either enable it or forbid it altogether. Thus the real control of the Internet derives not primarily from the DNS but from the fact that protocol itself is shaped by an altruistic, but nonetheless human and extra-protocological community.

Galloway argues that, "Life forms, both artificial and organic, exist in any space where material forces are actively aestheticized." I agree. But who is doing the aestheticizing? He continues, "The same protocological forces that regulate data flows within contingent environments such as distributed networks are the same forces that regulate matter itself." I'm not so sure. The forces that regulate "non-organic" "life" in network environments are protocols created by humans. The forces that regulate organic life in "natural" environments are material needs like food and shelter that are not created by humans (unless we're talking about a capitalistic environment, where many forces are man-made. But capitalism is not "matter itself.")

A reasonable string of questions thus arises: can vitality exist in economic and social systems apart from human life? Is Foucault's desire to "define a method of historical analysis freed from the anthropological theme" really viable? Does vitality exist in machinic systems without initial human input? There may be some minimal form of "vitality" on the network even without any humans actively using it (Eugene Thacker muses, "Is a network a network if it's not being used?"), but would that vitality exist without humans first constructing the network's protocol to begin with? Is individual human soulishness (mind, will, emotions) at the root of such vitality?

Even Tom Ray's "Tierra" (software that creates a virtual evolutionary environment in which "artificial lives" autonomously "live") still begins with human input. The "life" initially comes from Tom, and only indirectly from the protocol of the environment.

Strange Is Good

Protocol concludes on a less speculative, more balanced note. Galloway summarizes the problems inherent in protocol, and recognizes that its ethical use will ultimately depend on what we humans make of it.

The fact that I'm even able to dialogue with *Protocol* from a non-materialist, soulish perspective is testament to the solid, methodical, observational foundation Galloway has laid.

Personally, the chapters in *Protocol* on hacking, tactical media, and internet art make me excited to be making internet art in 2004. Not because *Protocol* extols the virtues of some futuristic AI utopia that's just around the bend (and has been just around the bend for the last 30 years without ever quite materializing), but because it exposes and delineates the very actual, sexy, dangerous shifts in media and culture currently underway. The truth is always stranger than fiction, and strange is good.

///

This review was originally published in *Rhizome Digest* (New York). Available online at <http://rhizome.org/discuss/view/13759/>.

2003
On Archiving, Ephemera, and Analog Distortion

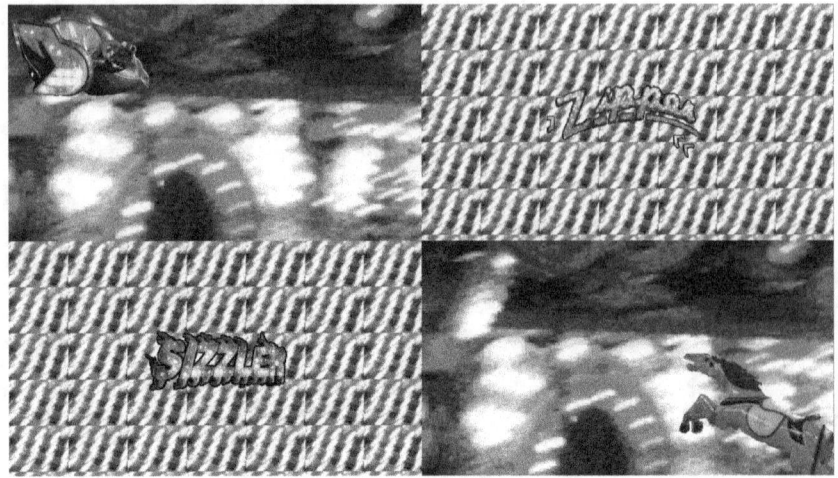

Curt Cloninger, *Playdamage #20 (Traveling Without Moving)*, playdamage.org/20.html, circa 2003. Courtesy of the artist.

According to Carrie Bickner, New York Public Library Assistant Director for Digital Information and System Design [1], digital archivists have two main concerns. The concern is not just with "bit integrity" (the integrity of the actual media being preserved); there exists the equally troublesome task of preserving the technology used to read the media. For example, my MS Word 2.0 document may be perfectly intact, but this does me no good if I no longer have any software that can read it.

Imagineer Danny Hillis looked into the problems of making a clock that would still be telling time thousands of years from now, and his best solution was to build a non-digital clock, trusting in the continuity of human culture to wind it physically as needed. [2]

But what if one relies on the peculiar quirks of a particular technology to create one's signature art? Where would Jimi Hendrix be without Marshall tube amp distortion? AmpFarm currently makes a digital Plug-In for Pro Tools that simulates the Hendrix amp set up, and the results are close, but no cigar.

Recently, Microsoft announced that it will no longer support Internet Explorer for the Mac. This means that all the Mac surfers currently using IE (a huge majority) will eventually migrate to something else, most likely Safari. And (as Nick Barker [3] recently pointed out) Safari does not support tiling animated gifs. To hardcore conceptual net artists and Action Script / Lingo/ Java net artists this is no big deal, but to a lo-fi dhtml net artist like myself, this failure is of some concern. It means that, for a potentially increasing number of visitors, the technology used to create some of the "art" of my "art" no longer functions desirably.

Not that Netscape 6 for Mac ever displayed tiling animated gifs "properly." It actually chokes on them, but in an interesting way. [4] But Safari doesn't even attempt to animate them. This is akin to the difference between analog and digital distortion. Analog distortion is messed up, but in a warm, gradual way that remains in dialogue with its source signal. It's a good thing. Digital distortion is binary. You either have a clear non-distorted signal, or a boring monotone clip that in no way resembles its source signal. Safari not animating the gifs at all is equivalent to this monotone clip.

To a hardcore conceptual artist for whom aesthetic craft is tangential fluff, my animated gif concerns are insipid. To a hardcore programmer coding abstract interactive vector shape environments, my animated gif concerns are obsolete. To a W3C-aware software developer at Safari, my concerns are ridiculous. But to a net.art archivist, my concerns are of potential interest. [5]

There is a legendary story about Led Zeppelin guitarist Jimmy Page that seems applicable. A rock journalist once asked Jimmy Page what rig he used (guitar, foot pedals, amp head, speakers) to get his signature tone. Page said, "I no longer answer that question publicly." Page went on to explain that he uses vintage equipment that's no longer newly manufactured. One time a few years ago, Page named the specific make and model of the equipment he used in an interview that was widely circulated in a major British publication. The next time Page's vintage equipment needed replacement parts, he went shopping around to vintage equipment dealers and pawn shops for the parts he needed, only to find that they were unaccountably sold out. Tons of young British guitarists had read the article and snatched up the remaining vintage equipment. Now their hero was no longer able to continue creating the original tone his fans were trying so hard to emulate.

This tale is usually told as a cautionary one regarding fame and mass media, but it also speaks of the ephemerality of the technology with which we develop our personal symbiotic relationships. Auriea Harvey [6] confided to me a couple of years ago that she was feeling like all the work she had done on the Web was in vain and lost. At the time, I thought she was over-reacting, temporarily burned out on the medium. Now, as browser companies crumble and the ephemerality of my early work becomes more apparent, I begin to understand a bit of what she was feeling.

The "solution" in commercial web design is, "code to standards." But if part of your art involves using non-standards code to "overdrive / break" standard browser rendering practices, then coding to standards is not always possible. Perhaps the solution is to embrace the ephemerality and just keep making new stuff. If that's the case, it could be argued that pimping one's own work becomes more important than ever. If people don't see it now, they won't be able to see it four years from now. The focus then shifts to the artist as public figure, and away from any single work itself. How many web designers revere Josh Davis without ever having seen early versions of www.once-upon-a-forest.com? How many net artists revere jodi without ever having seen early versions of www.jodi.org? Thus the net artists who "succeed" are those good at PR, good at branding themselves, good at coming up with projects that spin well and are viral, good at peppering the press with ongoing small projects instead of working for extended periods of time on larger, more meaningful projects.

Perhaps the solution is to pull an entropy8zuper – abandon the Net as an artistic medium altogether, go into hibernation for a year, and develop a grand narrative entertainment game that is neither net nor art. [7]

Or perhaps the solution is to keep working in the medium, dare to take on larger projects, [8] and then just not really care about what lasts or who sees it. Personally, I think I'm over the "who sees it" part (as much as any artist can be), but I'm surprised at how much the "what lasts" part is goading me.

///

This essay was originally published in *Intelligent Agent* (New York), and it's available online at <www.intelligentagent.com/archive/Vol3_No2_radical_cloningor.html>.

[1] Cf. <www.roguelibrarian.com>.
[2] Cf. <www.longnow.com> and <www.wired.com/wired/archive/6.05/hillis.html>.
[3] Cf. <www.nickbarker.org>.

[4] Surf <www.playdamage.org> on Mac N6 for examples.
[5] Cf. <https://web.archive.org/web/20090227071340/http://rhizome.org/artbase/policy.htm>, "appendix D: artist's intent".
[6] Cf. <www.e8z.org>.
[7] Cf. <www.tale-of-tales.com>.
[8] Perhaps making them modular, like <www.worldofawe.com> or <www.marrowmonkey.com>.

More References

Mark Tribe, "Archiving net.art", in *On Off,* June 2000, online at <www.afsnitp.dk/onoff/Texts/tribearchivingne.html>.

Steve Dietz, "Curating (on) the Web, Museums & the Web Conference", April 25, 1998. Online at <www.afsnitp.dk/onoff/Texts/dietzcuratingont.html>.

Anne-Marie Schleiner, "Fluidities and Oppositions among Curators, Filter Feeders, and Future Artists", in *intelligent agent*, vol. 3 no. 1, online at <www.intelligentagent.com/archive/Vol3_No1_curation_schleiner.html>.

Deep / Young Ethereal Archive, online at <www.deepyoung.org>.

2002

Signing In Tongues: DJ Spooky at the Emerald Lounge

DJ Spooky at Ars Electronica in 2003. © Ars Electronica Linz GmbH.

Rousseau walks on trumpet paths
Safaris to the heart of all that jazz
Through I-bars and girders, through wires and pipes
The mathematic circuits of the modern nights
Through huts, through Harlem, through jails and gospel pews
Through the class on Park and the trash on Vine
Through Europe and the deep deep heart of Dixie blue
Through savage progress cuts the jungle line
- Joni Mitchell

With only 30 people at the Emerald Lounge, and less than 15 people on the dance floor, DJ Spooky created the most spiritual live music I've heard since 1990, when the Kronos Quartet played Arvo Part's "Fratres" in Sewanee, Tennessee, and I was unable to speak afterwards for three hours. I was literally dumbstruck. Arvo Part had brought conviction; tonight DJ Spooky brought worship.

Critics compare Coltrane's late-era playing to speaking in tongues. For three hours, DJ Spooky was signing in tongues, like an ecstatic deaf person in the throes of some heavy supernatural experience, passionately trying to convey the unspeakable with his hands. The set was less cohesive than any of Coltrane's live 50+ minute jams. Instead, Spooky sounded more like a frenetic, [re]contextualizing Cecil Taylor – cultural commentary via syncopation.

I was unaccountably struck by the fact that DJ Spooky is a musician. Most DJ's rely on the musicianship of the artists they spin, letting the discs ride while they themselves focus on how not to mess up the next cut. Not Spooky. He was constantly busy, scratching discrete musical phrases as if he were playing an instrument (which, of course, he was). He wasn't just mixing and he wasn't just scratching, he was constructing new music.

DJ Spooky evinced an obvious intimacy with and appreciation of his source material, but it was not the appreciation that a collector has for his antique cars. It was more like the appreciation a carpenter has for his galvanized nails. This was "his" music. He didn't own it in the way contemporary Americans own land (in deed); he owned it in the way native Americans owned land (in relationship). Spooky's source material was a part of him, and he made himself a part of it as we listened.

Downtown
The dance halls and cafes
Feel so wild you could break somebody's heart
Just doing the latest dance craze
- Joni Mitchell

I dance like a freak. I stand in front of the speaker with the loudest bass, close my eyes, and assign different frequencies to specific parts of my body. I'm sure I look like an epileptic metalhead, but it doesn't really matter, because "we need body rockin, not perfection (let me get some action from the back section)." This "frequency-to-body-part" dance technique failed me several times tonight. At points, the mix got so dense with disparate intention, I was literally parylized. All I could do was stand there laughing and wait for the music to release me.

Not content to let any genre ride for more than five minutes, DJ Spooky took us on a tour of tabla funk, drum and bass, dub, reggae, house, and '80s electronica. I.M. Pei says of architecture, "I don't like 'isms.' Modernism, Classicism. To me it's just architecture." Tonight, it was just music.

If Cecil Taylor-esque in terms of literal hands-on business and exploration, Spooky proved a rudimentary Charles Mingus in terms of melodic/thematic composition. Most DJ's don't pay much mind to melody, but Spooky was tone-conscious, weaving melodic riffs and tropes while simultaneously tweaking their attendant backbeats.

The whole performance was permeated by DJ Spooky's overarching awareness that he is onto something new, relevant, and substantive. He was not DJ-ing, providing dance music, making art, scratching, mixing, or any single thing. He was celebrating the who/when/where of his existence. In that aspect, even though none of the music was overtly jazz-based, it felt like avant garde jazz. It was "in the moment" like an unforecastable Ornette Coleman jam. The discs themselves may have been time-shifted, but the music was live.

Shining hair and shining skin
Shining as she reeled him in
- Joni Mitchell

I left and drove the 20 minutes home crying most of the way. Through the mountains of western North Carolina, past the cow pastures and old barns and farm houses to my house in Dutch Cove, where my wife and kids are sleeping now. And I'm writing this in an attempt to do the show some kind of public justice before its inspiration dissolves into my own personal reservoir.

Because tonight, surrounded by redneck/hippie ravers drinking moonshine and dancing contrived, I experienced the real deal. Someone was birthing something living and risky and celebratory in the midst of our timid, detatched, stillborn, contemporary coprus. I could feel it; I saw it shining; and it made me move.

///

This review was originally posted to *Rhizome Raw* (New York). <http://rhizome.org/discuss/view/12455/>. The reported event took place at Asheville, North Carolina from Sunday Night, August 18, to Monday Morning, August 19, 2002.

2001

Lurkin' in the Murk: a Unified Theory of Cognisance

The Olivia Tremor Control. Image via nrgm.fi.

This is actually not a unified theory of cognisance, but an attempt to synthesize several different paths of study I've been pursuing. Source material includes: *Kant and the Platypus: Essays on Language and Cognition*, by Umberto Eco; *Understanding Comics* by Scott

McCloud; *The Man Who Tasted Shapes* by Richard C. Cytowic; *Black Foliage* by Olivia Tremor Control; and *Astral Week*s by Van Morrison.

Eco describes a phase of gradual comprehension prior to the point of "naming." By the time we say, "I saw a dog," we've already gone through several levels of recognition, categorization, and abstraction. But before any of this naming happens, there is an object that exists which has somehow attracted our attention to the exclusion of all the other existing objects that could have attracted our attention. Eco describes this object as an impressor, a cast-maker. We are the "impresee"s, the clay into which the "impressor" object presses. The impression, the cast or mold that results from this encounter, is the icon. It is what we consider the object to be. It is not the object (cf. René Magritte's *La Trahison des Images*, 1929). This icon is an impression of the object, created by the object, and thus defined by the absence of the object. In binary terms, the object is 1, and the icon is 0. Presence and absence.

So icons, signs, words, and symbols are the 0's created by a real world full of 1's. As we turn these icons into art and transmit them via media, these icons become objects in and of themselves. An image on my web site is no longer an impression on my mind; it is now an object that can leave an impression on someone else's mind. So I've taken my 0's and turned them into 1's. Dreams made real. And when people visit my site, my site makes an impression, a 0, on them.

If I take an analog cassette tape and record it, and then I record the recording, then I record the recording of the recording, the quality of the audio on that tape is going to degenerate pretty quickly. It's like the "secrets" game where you whisper something to someone, and then they pass it on, and on and on. In the end, the message invariably gets distorted.

So as the creator of a web site (or of any art), I have the opportunity to intentionally throw my own distortion into the remix process. Actually, since I'm passing on my impression of the primary object rather than the object itself, I will necessarily re-interpret it and re-mix it. I've got an impression, a cast, an empty shell, an outline in my mind created by an object in the world. When I make art, I attempt to reverse the concavity of that void, and throw its dimensions out into convex reality. Whatever corners or edges or niches in the initial impression were vague or hazy must necessarily be given dimension by me if my newly created convex "1" is going to be able to stand up on its own in a world of objects. In the transition between memory and art, information is necessarily lost. Oftentimes the craft of "art" simply comes down to the ability to minimize (or at least creatively control) the amount of information lost during this transitional process. To quote Lou Reed, "Between thought and expression there lies a lifetime."

Cytowic suggests that everybody receives sense impressions on a synesthetic, pre-sensory (or proto-sensory) plane. In other words, as color travels through my eye, before my brain is able to abstract it as "sight," it perceives it simply as "sense." The same with taste, touch, smell, and sound. All these sense impressions "occur" to our minds first in raw form, and only later (albeit milliseconds later) are they hierarchized into comfortably "recognizable" sensory impressions. I find it interesting that both Eco (coming from a semiotic perspective) and Cytowic (coming from a quasi-neurological perspective) both identify a pre-cognisant arena of first sense. Both authors speak of this pre-cognisant arena with delicacy, reverence,

and awe. It is the rich, totally experiential and visceral ground from which all human knowing and understanding are abstracted.

Words derive from this pre-cognisant arena, but this arena itself is a-verbal. All art "speaks" in this arena first, and then on and up it goes. Most concrete art strongly influences its viewer to move away from this vague murky area of first perception and on to higher areas of understanding, categorizing, and naming. A crisp, clear, photograph of a shiny new car is a crisp, clear, photograph of a shiny new car. It insists that we perceive it as such. But what if one could make art that was so vague in its representational intent that it invited the viewer to remain in this fecund, pre-cognisant arena of existence? We can't even refer to this arena as a state of "understanding," or a state of "appreciation," or a state of "interpretation," because to speak of it in such concrete terms belies the fact that mental abstraction has already been made, in which case the viewer has moved on up the path of knowledge, they are no longer "lurking in the murk." To even call this pre-cognisant arena a "state" is dicey, because a state connotes stasis, and this is an arena that is by definition "pre-." You don't stay in pre-cognisance; you pass through it (and pretty darned quickly according to Eco, Peirce, Kant, et. al.) To even refer to this pre-cognisant arena of firstness in any way at all is to cause it to evaporate. Like sub-atomic particle physics. Once you know where the electrons are, you've lost the ability to know how fast they are moving. So too with pre-cognisance. Once you call this transition murk "the pre-cognisant arena," it's clear that you've already passed through said arena and are now looking back down on it from the cozy heights of cognition.

But I don't claim to be writing this essay from a pre-cognisant state. I'm just saying that such a state exists. Furthermore, I'm saying that

as we make art, we are able to create a primary object (albeit a once-removed, mediated object) which, when presented to a viewer, will cause an impression on that viewer that forces him to travel through this pre-cognisant state and on toward knowledge. What if, as artists, when we turn our concave 0's (our sense impressions) into convex 1's (our art objects), we push these impressions out into reality in an intentionally vague, non-specific way, a way which barely distinguishes between our impressions and our art objects.

To extend the analogy, let's say I see a dog. (Already the sentence "I see a dog" puts me farther down the spectrum of understanding than I want to be, but I've got to use language, so bear with me.) As this "dog object impressor" begins "impressing" me, it pushes its way in first gradually and non-distinctly. What if I immediately turn my attention away from the dog the split-second after it begins to impress me? Were I to then return in my mind to the memory of that aborted impression, it would have only pressed in on me a bit. Interesting. What if I continue looking at the dog, letting it impress in all the way, and then I return in my mind and memory to the beginnings of this "impressing" event? What if I determine to whittle down all of the distinct and clear impressions that the dog has ultimately made on me, and I simply retain the impression of the beginnings of my contact with the dog object?

Now, what if I take that vague initial impression, that primordial icon, that blurry 0, that shallow hole, and push it back out into reality by making it art? Now my art object, my tangible 1, is nothing more than an unformed mound. Any person on whom that mound makes an impression will not be impressed too concretely. They will not perceive "dog" in any concrete, highly abstracted "knowledgeable" way. They will perceive the beginnings of my experience. I will

have forced them to perceive these murky beginnings by not giving them anything beyond the beginnings. "Rational" art patrons will try in vain to abstract my rudimentary pre-cognisant art to higher levels of "knowing" and "naming," but my art will thwart their attempts to do this by not giving them enough information with which to work, and they will dismiss my art as meaningless.

But other patrons will recognize my art as familiar. "Hey, this is the place I always pass through on my way to recognizing and labelling a dog. I remember this place. Boy, who on earth would have ever thought to stop and document here?" Such patrons will "get" our art.

Furthermore, according to the principles set forth by McCloud in *Understanding Comics*, the web is set up by its very nature to present a pre-cognisant world; a world that exists at the boundary where objects become words; a world that exists at the divide where raw sense impressions are parsed into sound, sight, and touch. Web art presents a "1" object, but not a very concrete one. Web art presents a "1" of light, sound, and shifting sand. It pushes on our minds, and our minds give. We push on the interactive art, and it gives. Web art has the ability to leave a shallow primordial footprint. Web art invites us to lurk in the pre-cognisant murk.

Olivia Tremor Control states, "We will find a way to animate the sounds we feel inside." They wonder, "How can we liberate the world of sound?" They confide, "You are the subject of sketches I've made for a sculptured sound." The Olivia Tremor Control is a band attempting to push their shallow 0 into a blunt 1.

By referring to this pre-cognisant impression stage as "shallow" and "vague," I am forced to perjoratize it. "Shallow" and "vague" sound derogatory. Such is the tyranny of language, which surely

has a predisposed bias against such a pre-linguistic state. (Which explains why Eco is so danged difficult to read!) But "shallow" is also thousands of miles wide, and "vague" is also full of thousands of possible meanings. Furthermore, such art need not be blurry and abstract. It can be iconic and crisp a la Dalì. A human fetus is on its way to becoming an adult, but a snap shot of a fetus need not be blurry. You can take a very clear and crisp picture of a primordial state. It just might look a bit strange.

Such pre-cognisant web art needs not exclude words. Indeed, there are some genius artists so skilled at hacking and reverse-engineer words, that they use even these enemies of pre-cognisance to create wonderfully blunt and resonant art objects. Neil Young, Paul Simon, Emily Dickinson – if they can invoke pre-cognisance using mere words, surely we can invoke it via the multi-sensory arsenal of web media. I'll leave you with one such primordial lyric, and an invitation to join me in surfing the murk:

If I ventured in the slipstream
Between the viaducts of your dreams
Where the mobile steel rims crack
And the ditch and the backroads stop
Could you find me
Would you kiss my eyes
And lay me down
In silence easy
To be born again

- Van Morrison

///

This essay was originally published in *spark-online (Vancouver). Available online at <www.spark-online.com/february01/discourse/cloninger.html>.

2000

Usability Experts Are From Mars, Graphic Designers Are From Venus

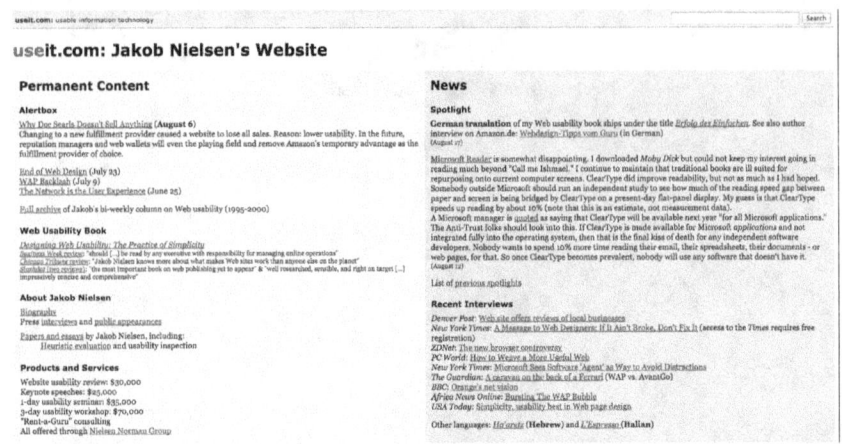

useit.com front page in August 2000

There is an unarticulated war currently raging among those who make web sites. Like the war between dark- and light-skinned blacks in Spike Lee's *School Daze*, this conflict is one that only its participants recognize. The war is not between commercial sites and experimental sites. It's not between "Bloggers" and "Flashers." This war is between usability experts and graphic designers.

In the usability corner, wearing the blue and purple underlined trunks, weighing in at just under 25K per gig... J-a-a-a-a-a-kob Nie-e-e-e-e-lsen, usability guru extroadinaire, with over 16 usability patents and several "lists of 10" – do's, don't's, thou shalt's, and thou shalt not's.

And in the graphic design corner, wearing the greyscale trunks, weighing in at 500K per site (that's dollars, not bytes)... Kioken(oken-oken-oken), firing clients left and right, and wielding Flash as if the plug-in itself were built into Joe Newbie's genetic makeup.

Nielsen thinks today's web is an advanced but ill-used database. Kioken thinks today's web is a fledgling but ill-used multimedia platform. And each side KNOWS that their view of the web will prevail. Observe the (over)confidence. Nielsen:

"Boo.com has closed. Good riddance. Boo was one of the very few high-profile sites to launch in recent months that dared violate my design principles and aim for glitz rather than usability... It proves that overly fancy design doesn't work."

Gene Na (co-founder of Kioken):

"We had to fire Sony the other week. They weren't listening to us, so we let them go. We actually had to get rid of Bad Boy [Entertainment] in the beginning, but they straightened up and came back. So did Sony. What the client sometimes doesn't understand is the less they talk to us, the better it is. We know what's best."

Let the celebrity death match begin. Gentlemen, I expect a good clean fight. Come out with your hands up, and may the best web paradigm win.

What's So Funny About Peace, Love, and Understanding?

I wager that after 15 rounds, after broadband, after standards compliance, after the increasingly mythical release of Netscape 6, both the usability experts and the graphic designers will still be standing. The web is just too big for one paradigm to prevail. Some sites will need intensive whiz-bang branding that Nielsen's "principles" won't allow. Other sites will need moronically basic navigation and speedy download times that Kioken doesn't care to provide. Most sites will need some combination thereof. So why the war? Why can't the usability experts and the graphic designers just love each other?

For better or worse, the divide between these two camps existed long before "new media," and will continue to exist long after the web has become as commonplace as indoor plumbing. "New media" merely brings this dichotomy into renewed focus because, well, it's new. We're still developing the web's vocabulary. Consequently, we're still trying to get a handle on this "usability/design" conundrum, largely unaware of its primordial origins. With that in mind, allow me to glibly and over-simplistically delineate the situation:

Usability/ Information Architecture = the masculine = the left side of the brain = doing = math/science = the rational = logical action = the articulatable = Mars.

Graphic Design = the feminine = the right side of the brain = being = art = the emotional = intuitive action = the inarticulatable = Venus.

It's no surprise then, that Master Nielsen makes most of his dough writing and talking (the articulatable), whereas Kioken makes most of their dough designing (the inarticulatable). Indeed, to re-quote Na, "the less the client TALKS to us, the better it is."

You can see why each group would quickly get on the other's nerves. The usability experts find the graphic designers too touchy feely. "What do they mean they need to mess around with the look and feel to see what develops? Why can't they just give me a wireframe now?" The graphic designers find the usability experts too

blunt and by-the-book. "What do they mean graphics are just the icing on the cake? Without graphic design, all you've got is a plan!"

Meta-Voodoo Usability

In the press and on the bulletin boards, the graphic designers tend to take a beating. And not surprisingly. They are the inarticulate ones, remember? Thus you get articles that malign innovative designers without rightly discerning the purpose of their sites; or worse, you get outright dreck written by blind guides who wouldn't know aesthetic appeal if it stripped bare and gave them a table dance.

But wait, the usability experts have their statistics! It has been documented! The users are on their side! But what questions are these usability studies asking? "Could you find it?" "Were you able to accomplish it?" "Articulate to us IN WORDS what you were able to DO." Such questions presuppose a "Martian" criterion for user experience. If the site is a "Martian" site (logical, rational, left-brained), then it will score well on Nielsen's usability test. If the site is a "Venusian" site (intuitive, emotional, right-brained), then it will score poorly on Nielsen's usability test. Were Nielsen to ask his subjects, "Write a short essay on how this site made you feel," he would get dramatically different statistical results. But of course, testing like that would be touchy-feely and unscientific. To use his own jargon then, Nielsen-esque usability testing is, in the overall scheme of things, yet another form of "voodoo" usability. It finds what it is looking for and ignores what it is unable to measure.

But what if Levis doesn't have a huge database of products that it's selling online? What if Levis just wants people to feel that its

vintage clothing is rugged and somewhat extreme? What if a successful site to Levis is a site that conveys an emotion, an attitude, a world-view? In other words, what if Levis is branding? Most usability tests are impotent to evaluate the success of a site in terms of conveyed emotion, because emotion is something that most users (and most humans) have difficulty articulating, particularly in response to multiple choice questions. But just because a positive interactive experience can't be charted doesn't mean it hasn't occurred.

I Am The Lorax, I Speak for the Trees

The graphic designers sense that something is amiss, yet they are largely tongue-tied in their efforts to refute "the violence inherent in the system." Being young, punkish, rebellious youths (all tattooed, shorn, and pierced to the hilt as well), they lash out blindly, saying ill-conceived, inarticulate, un-endearing things. Thus Sr. Nielsen scores even more opportunities to indoctrinate the corporate movers and shakers, while an entire subculture of frustrated designers churns away in obscurity, thrashing their anti-capitalistic design statements into the cyber-void.

Until now. The graphic design community is finally getting some poster boys: Kioken's Joshua Davis, VolumeOne's Matt Owens, Juxt Interactive's Todd Purgason, and a host of other thoughtful professionals who are crafting graphic-intensive commercial sites that big clients are finding increasingly hard to resist.

The theorists and writers advocating graphic web design have been a little slower to emerge (for reasons already belabored above). Graphic design doesn't exactly lend itself to a specific list of do's

and don't's. User interface jedi Nathan Shedroff has a wonderfully conceived piece on interface seduction [1], but it's still mighty
abstract. I've come up with my own list of ten fresh design styles
[2], which I hope is a step toward developing a more articulate web
design vocabulary. And there is always the odd enlightened piece
on graphic design from a classic "list of 10" perspective.

But writers about graphic design will never have as many easily articulatable "principles" as Jakob Nielsen (if they do, beware).
Such inarticulatability is inherent to a vocabulary of the aesthetic.
Graphic design on the web is no exception. Still, just because a truth
can't be reduced to a sound bite, it nevertheless remains a truth.

I've Looked at Clouds from Both Sides Now

Although the web began as a medium to exchange physics research papers, it seems naive to expect it to remain predominately
text-based. Usability experts bemoan the evolution of the web into
something beyond a card catalog. Their "speedy download" mantras
belie their reluctance to jettison a word-based web. But just because
the web was born in text doesn't mean it need remain in text.

CD-ROMs were born in gaming, and now the CD-ROM medium includes encyclopedias, experimental ambient environments,
and virtual cookbooks. You don't hear old-school game designers
saying, "The William Sonoma Guide to Fine Cooking CD-ROM is a
total crock! There's not even a hint of competition! We all know that
CD-ROMs are by their very nature competitive!" How ludicrous.
Yet there are still old-school usability experts saying, "Don't they
know the web is about accessing information? Who cares what it

looks like? Where's the content?"

I don't think the web is going to turn into interactive TV, but neither will it remain a forum for exchanging physics outlines. And who wants it to, anyway? For all their statistics, arguments, and lists, the usability experts are overlooking the fact that we, as humans, are not all Martians. Indeed, there is a little Venus in us all, and some of us are nothing but Venusian.

Yes, I admonish all graphic designers to heed the few user interface experts who bother to critique your flash layouts without blindly dismissing your entire site. [3]

But usability gurus, heed ye the words of hippy sage Joni Mitchell as she describes the mechanics of human interaction:

Rows and flows of angel hair,
Ice cream castles in the air,
Feather canyons everywhere,
I've looked at clouds that way.
But now they only block the sun.
They rain, they snow on everyone.
So many things I would've done
But clouds got in my way.
I've looked at clouds from both sides now,
From up and down and still somehow
It's clouds' illusions I recall.
I really don't know clouds at all.

Substitute "graphic design" for "clouds" and you get the idea. Unless usability experts are willing to admit that a 250K streaming flash file may indeed be the best solution for a branding site's core page, those same experts may find themselves expounding in exile on Mars while the rest of us humans intuit the neo-web experience.

///

This essay was originally published in *A List Apart* (New York). Available online at
<http://alistapart.com/article/marsvenus>.

[1] Cf. <www.nathan.com/thoughts/seduction/>.
[2] Cf. <www.lab404.com/dan/>.
[3] Cf. <www.flazoom.com/news/fitts_07102000.shtml>.

LINK Editions

http://editions.linkartcenter.eu/

Clouds

Domenico Quaranta, *In Your Computer,* 2011
Valentina Tanni, *Random,* 2011
Gene McHugh, *Post Internet,* 2011
Brad Troemel, *Peer Pressure,* 2011
Kevin Bewersdorf, *Spirit Surfing,* 2012
Mathias Jansson, *Everything I shoot Is Art,* 2012
Domenico Quaranta, *Beyond New Media Art*, 2013
Curt Cloninger, *One Per Year*, 2014

In My Computer

#1 Miltos Manetas, *In My Computer*, 2011
#2 Chris Coy, *After Brad Troemel*, 2013
#3 Martin Howse, *Diff in June*, 2013
#4 Damiano Nava, *Let the Right One In*, 2013
#5 Evan Roth, *Since You Were Born*, 2014
#6 Addie Wagenknecht, *Technological Selection of Fate*, 2014

Catalogues

Collect the WWWorld. The Artist as Archivist in the Internet Age, 2011.
Exhibition catalogue. Edited by Domenico Quaranta, with texts by Josephine Bosma, Gene McHugh, Joanne McNeil, D. Quaranta

Gazira Babeli, 2011.
Exhibition catalogue. Edited by Domenico Quaranta, with texts by Mario Gerosa, Patrick Lichty, D. Quaranta, Alan Sondheim

Holy Fire. Art of the Digital Age, 2011.
Exhibition catalogue, edited by Yves Bernard, Domenico Quaranta

Ryan's Web 1.0. A Lossless Fall, 2012.
By Ryan Trecartin

RE:Akt! Reconstruction, Re-enactment, Re-reporting, 2014.
Exhibition Catalogue. Edited by Antonio Caronia, Janez Janša, Domenico Quaranta, with texts by Jennifer Allen, Jan Verwoert, Rod Dickinson.

Born Digital, 2014.
Exhibition Catalogue. Edited by Link Art Center.

Open

Best of Rhizome 2012, 2013.
Edited by Joanne McNeil
Co-produced with Rhizome, New York (USA).

The F.A.T. Manual, 2013.
Edited by Geraldine Juárez, Domenico Quaranta.
Co-produced with MU, Eindhoven (NL).

Troika, 2013.
Edited by Domenico Quaranta
Co-produced with Aksioma - Institute for Contemporary Art, Ljubljana (SLO).